My Invincible Life

Andrea Dawn Driver

Copyright © 2019 by Awakenings with Andrea Dawn

All rights reserved. This book, in whole or in part, may not be reproduced in any form, stored in any retrieval system, or transmitted in any form by any means—electronic, mechanical, photocopy, recording, or otherwise—without prior written permission of the publisher, except as allowed under U.S. 'fair use' law.

The content of this memoir is written from my own experiences and point of view. Conversations and events are based on my best recollection and are being told in a way that evoke the feeling and meaning of what was said or transpired and, in all instances, the essence of the dialogue or event is accurate. Some names and identifying details may have been changed to protect the privacy of individuals.

This book is not intended to provide legal, psychological, medical, financial, business, or other advice or treatments. My intent is only to offer information of a general nature on what has helped me on my quest for emotional and spiritual well-being. In the event you use any of the information in this book for yourself, I do not assume any responsibility for your actions. You must seek professional medical advice from your Healthcare or Service Professional if you have any health, psychological, or emotional concerns.

Manufactured in the United States of America, or in the United Kingdom when distributed elsewhere.

Driver, Andrea Dawn

>My Invincible Life
>ISBN: 9780578575636

Cover design: Natasha Clawson
Copy editing: Claudia Volkman
Additional copy editing: Rebecca Driver

Please visit my website at AwakeningsWithAndreaDawn.com.

Contents

Contents 2
Dedication 5
Prologue 6
Foreword 8
PART ONE: My Invincible Truth 10
  Why Be Normal? 10
  The Beginning 12
  The Beginning of the Beginning 15
  Dad 18
  Mom 21
  Crazy Freedom 25
  The Falsehood of Adulthood 30
  Sex, Drugs, and Violence 33
    Back to life on the funny farm 40
  A New Beginning 51
  Out on My Limb 59
  Crazy Self Love 69
  Conclusion 74
PART TWO: My Invincible Awakening 77
  Introduction 77
  Getting From Here to There 78
  Manifesting for Prosperity 80
  Discovering Rituals 83
    Water 84
    Essential Oils 84

- Morning Prayer/Meditation 85
- Crystals and Stones 86
- Jewelry 86
- Music 87
- Before Sleep Relaxation 87
- Baths 88

Overcoming Judgment, Shame, and Guilt 91
Maintaining Vibrational Frequency 96
Releasing Addiction to Comfort 99
My Sexual Awakening 102
Conclusion 107

PART THREE: My Invincible Love 110
Introduction 110
Pure Love 112
- The Apostle John 113
- Seshemi, Daughter of Setankhu – Thirteenth Dynasty 116

Truth 120
- The Apostle Paul 121
- Acts 9:3-20 New International Version (NIV) 123
- The Apostle Peter 126

Choices 130
There Is No Pain 134
- A Message from Muhammed: 137

Noticing and Synchronicity 141
Freedom & Followership 143
- Channeled with Jesus and the Apostles 143

Conclusion 144

Epilogue 146
A Final Channeling 151
   The Ursula 151
References..154
Books That Have Added Awareness to My Life 155

Dedication

This book is dedicated to all of humanity. It's time to share our stories. There are so many of us that have endured trauma and it is time to come together to end the cycle.

This is for anyone who has experienced mental, emotional abuse, trauma, sexual assault, rape and any or all other traumas. It has been written to bring hope to your life, so you, too, can share your story.

Prologue

Each of us is on a life journey. Depending on our cultural, spiritual, academic or personal beliefs we may each refer to this life journey differently. In the works following, I will frequently use the words love, soul, spirituality, and spiritual awakening to explain my own experiences around my personal growth.

In my journey as a child, rebellious teenager, wife, mother, employee, business owner, spiritual alchemist, psychic medium, and channeler, I have met so many people who are searching for answers. What they don't realize is that the answers do not reside in messages from others. You see, the answers always lie within. The energy is rising within Mother Earth; all around us, there is a need coming from within to make change, to follow our path that we set out to do before we were born.

Our shared experiences create the defining hook; the hook that attaches to a part of us, telling us we are stuck on a line, trapped and unfulfilled. When we try to break away, the hook easily gets caught on something else, a constant reminder that we are not free. Like you, I am continually working to unhook from old beliefs and become the best version of myself that I know to be.

Some of us want the full details of one's life story, while others want a guidebook for living a best life. This book does not promise to be either of those; I do commit to share my personal truth, to awakening, to love.

To get the most from this book experience, you may not want to read the book in its entirety. Each of the three segments has its own unique message.

You may have picked it up solely to find a single bit of truth that speaks most to your heart.

You are encouraged to go directly to the segment that resonates.

- ➢ My Invincible Truth: My life from the beginning on through to a memory that changed my life. This part of the book is graphic and not for the faint of heart.

- ➢ My Invincible Awakening: The rituals and practices that I use to stay completely in tune with my soul's truth.

- ➢ My Invincible Love: Channeled messages describing what we most need to know about love.

I had been helpless and I had to gain understanding from hurts that were long hidden. The trauma was immense. Yet, through all the discomfort I found myself. And in finding myself, I share my story of triumph to help others, like you, to see deep within their souls to discover their best selves, their glorious selves.

May you continue to be blessed on your own life journey.

Foreword

When I was sixteen years old looking up at the stars wondering whether I should end my life and whether there was a God, I was given a vision of helping others. I remember thinking, "if I do live, it will be to help other people in my situation." The statement came through me with such conviction, I knew it would come true. I did not, however, in that moment or anytime over the following couple of decades, ever imagine writing a book. Then, in 2014 I was shown three books and given an urge to share my story. It was told to me that the book would be the way for me to help other people as shown in the vision decades before.

Thus, in the pages that follow, you will find the story of 'My Invincible Life.' A biography of childhood, marriage, mothering, psychic awakening, and spiritual messages. A story of surviving a chaotic childhood by learning to thrive and celebrate every part of the journey. In the beginning I was shown three books and when I started the writing process the first theme to reveal itself was that of a messy childhood. The second theme was the story of my awakening. The third was an evolved understanding of love that transcends coupled relationships and spans across all of humanity. Over the course of three years it took to write this book, those three books merged as three sub-sections of one book.

If you have picked up this book you have been invited into my life and I thank you for joining me in a time of discovery about myself, my awakening to spirituality and the divine love that is available for everyone. The sections have been written in such a way that they can stand alone. Thus, if you just want to read about a chaotic childhood read 'My Invincible Truth.' If you are searching for examples of activities one might engage in for a spiritual awakening read 'My Invincible Awakening.' If you want to discover perspectives on life and love from spiritual messengers read 'My Invincible Love.' Or, if you'd like to laugh, cry and celebrate life of a thriving woman read the entire journey of 'My Invincible Life.'

Whatever parts of this book you choose, please remember that it is only my story. It is not to be interpreted as legal, psychological, medical, financial, business or other advice or treatments. It is written to be fun, entertaining and enlightening. Look for the parts that LIGHTEN your heart, make you feel good and offer insights specific to your own well-being. If you find a section that contradicts your own belief system, please skip it and let it go. Any message that does not feel true for you, was not meant for you. My conviction at age 16 was to share my story only for the purpose of giving others hope. So, if you take away anything from this book, take away hope. Take away that belief that you can help yourself through any situation and always remember that love is the way forward.

With Invincible Love,

Andrea Dawn

PART ONE: My Invincible Truth

Why Be Normal?

We are all weird in some way. When we hide who we are, we suffer. Don't suffer ... be free.

This book chronicles sex, drugs, divorce, dysfunction, homeschooling, rape, molestation, and spirituality. My story is not better or worse than anybody else's; it just is. I am not a role model and am by no means perfect. I am just ready to fully share my truth.

There is nothing that we can't overcome.

From the outside looking in, people have always thought I was a bit weird. So I quickly learned how to be a chameleon, to mask the very things that made me unique. What was so weird? When I would share what was happening in my head, or in my family, or with other kids, it was difficult for others to understand. Whenever I shared parts of my story, kids would even say things like, "You're really crazy." As a kid, I looked at being different as a matter-of-fact. I couldn't be who I was because who I was didn't fit the norm.

Despite my weirdness, I was actually remarkably good at fitting in when needed. When I look back now, it is easy to see that all of it was happening for a reason, and that reason was here to support me. While it was happening, though, I really believed I was crazy because I could see and hear things others couldn't. My family looked different from my peers' families, and my authentic self was hidden under fear.

My life was filled with chaos, uncertainty, and pain. It was also filled with kindness, love, and divine guidance. I went from thinking I was crazy and hiding it by pretending I wasn't, to accepting that my craziness is really my invincible truth. Now, I love every bit of it.

Almost everybody is afraid to be their authentic self. Throughout my life, I have learned who, how, and what I am. The truth is I am a divine soul, a daughter, a sister, a friend, a spiritual alchemist, and a go-between of this dimension and other dimensions. Whatever I'm called to be, I now do this without fear, hesitation, or insecurity.

Mediumship, spirituality, and intuition are the things that I tried so hard to hide, and now they make up my livelihood. I think you, my reader, are here because some part of my story is also a part of yours. Perhaps because, in some way, we all have a little crazy in each of us, and playing it safe doesn't create safety. Maybe you are curious about how a person goes from extreme dysfunction to fully expressed spirituality. Maybe you see visions, hear voices, or feel the emotions of others. I want you to have an amazing sense of wonder and freedom in every aspect of your life. Imagine what it might be like to be totally, completely, and wonderfully crazy you!

When you read parts of my story, you may wonder how I could be okay, and the answer is simple: We're all okay. There is nothing we walk through that doesn't heal. Every step we take is just a part of the journey. It is neither a beginning nor an end. It is just a part of it. As you read this, please don't only focus on the dysfunction or trauma. Instead, look for the depth of love, the joy, and the miracles continuing to emerge not just in my life, but in all of our lives.

The Beginning

When I was five years old, I can remember meeting my deceased grandfather in my bedroom and having a conversation with him. At that time, I was already hearing voices in my head.

I was also growing up in a dysfunctional home, and my great-grandmother and my mom used to talk about how crazy my grandmother was. I remember telling myself that if they heard the voices in my head, they would think I was crazier than Grandma, so I never said anything to anybody about my experiences with Spirit. I went through my wild teen years, got married at twenty, and had three daughters who soon became my whole life. For the next twenty years, I only knew myself as a mom and wife.

In late 2012, I had a memory recall that I was sexually abused. I went to a counselor for several months, and there I realized I needed to find myself—I didn't have any idea who I was. I thanked the counselor for everything she had done, and I began to recognize that the past was just that: the past. It was behind me, and I could only move forward.

I began a journey then, one that led me to some self-help type seminars. Through all of this, I was accompanied by my friend and carpool buddy, JennMarie, because she was also going through some changes. Carpooling together is something we had been doing daily for years. We talked through everything; nothing was left to the imagination, and we held nothing back.

JennMarie and I in 2013

JennMarie invited me to a class at a spirituality center. I didn't want to go because I was a Christian, and I wanted to stay with the traditional Bible-based study that was helping me keep my marriage together along with my sanity. As we were carpooling, she would read from the course books and continuously urge me to go to at least one class.

Eventually, after hearing some of the wisdom being shared, I agreed and went to a class with JennMarie. During the class, the reverend began talking about a dear friend of hers who had passed. As she continued talking about him, the left side of my body started to go wonky. At first, I felt as if I couldn't move my leg, but the sensation passed. Then, I felt the numbness in my arm, my chest, and my neck. I realized that I was experiencing what a stroke would feel like, but I knew I wasn't actually having a stroke because there was no pain. After the class was over, I walked up to Reverend Patti and asked if her friend had died from a stroke.

She said, "Why, yes, why do you ask?"

"No reason," I responded, and with a freaky feeling, I turned around and walked away as fast as I could. JennMarie and I talked about it all the way home. The next week came, and we were sitting in class, again listening to Reverend Patti talk about the course books. It was as though a light switch went on, and I started hearing all kinds of voices, just like when I was a child. I remember thinking, *Oh my gosh, I really am crazy. This is just like when I was five.* I tried ignoring the voices, but one particular male voice started coming in strongly and began telling me things about someone in the class. This was not a person I was close to and, quite frankly, I really had no curiosity about. But I was hearing details about her life, and I felt confused. *Am I making this stuff up? Why I am thinking about this? Who is this male voice?* As I was hearing this voice, I was also arguing with myself to get the transmission of information to stop. After class, I told JennMarie what had happened. She looked at me and said matter-of-factly, "Maybe you can talk with those who have crossed over."

Hearing those words, my life flashed before my eyes, and I was shown many instances where I had unknowingly been communicating with Spirit. The unexplained was being explained. JennMarie had a number of loved ones who had passed away over the years, so I began connecting her with these people on the other side. We talked with a friend who was suspected of taking his own life, and we learned that the death was accidental.

This opened the door for even more crossed-over friends and loved ones to start coming through during the carpooling. I then began to practice this on my own. Through friends, colleagues, and referrals, a new life featuring my spiritual connection blossomed.

The Beginning of the Beginning

Does an idyllic childhood have a single-story home in a lovely neighborhood? Does it have two parents who love each other? Does it have stability? Goodness knows my family didn't have any of those things. Yet I can't help but wonder, if I'd had all those things, would I still be my crazy self?

I believe in something called soul contracts. These are agreements we make before we are born to achieve significant growth in our human form. They play an important role for everyone with whom we come in contact. My life is filled with an abundance of soul contracts in the form of family. My family consists of so many different people (parents, siblings, step-parents, step-siblings) that I had to draw a diagram just to make sure I didn't forget anyone! All these various family members also explain why chaos felt more comfortable to me than stability. To me, chaos was fun, dramatic, and unpredictable.

I'll start at the beginning to give you a better understanding of how and why I came to love the chaos. Once upon a time ... well, it does feel like a very long time ago ... I came into this world with such a roar that the hospital actually kicked me out for being too loud. Apparently, my cacophony was just a little bit too much for all the other newborns and caused a ruckus, so they asked my mom to leave the day after I came into this world. In those days, new moms got to stay in the hospital for three days, so leaving after the first day was a big deal.

My mom and dad were not together very long after having me. There were problems from the start, considering it was only meant to be a one-night stand. However, something else happened: my older sister. She was born nine months after my parents' one-night stand and three years before me. My dad didn't see her until she was almost six months old. They tried to make a relationship work, and then I came along. Who knows why they had me! They were such opposites, it makes me wonder how they got together in the first place. A bit like Marilyn

Monroe and Arthur Miller—there was some kind of attraction, but the rest of the world sat in wonder, scratching their heads.

By the time I was two years old, my parents had split and went on their marry ways (yes, I mean *marry*) to their second relationships. Their relationship ended badly, and a custody battle ensued. My dad and his second wife got married secretly so he could show the judge he was the better parent. My mother followed suit with her own marriage about a month later.

My dad's new marriage came with two more daughters that he eventually adopted. That meant four girls, ages two, three, four, and five. In the end, my mom won custody. Unfortunately, this maternal bias is still typical today, even if the mother is not fit to take care of the kids. I was four years old when the custody decision was finalized, and the following year, my mom and first stepdad had a son together, my only brother.

Me and my three sisters

My biological dad is a source of stability in my life, even today. He was a librarian and has remained so for my whole life. He worked in a few different libraries before he ultimately retired. My dad and my stepmom divorced when I was eleven years old. Dad then found his third wife when I was fifteen years old, and they have been married ever since. She was a librarian too, so I can see where my love of reading comes from.

My biological mom, on the other hand, showed me how to live a life of chaos. She worked odd jobs before settling into a job at a phone company for ten years. When she retired from there, she again took various jobs. In 1981, my mom divorced my stepdad (husband number two) and didn't remarry until 2000. She has since divorced husband number three and married husband number four. Each of Mom's relationships was dramatically different from the previous one. She partied hard for years before she was "saved" and embraced Christianity.

Even though my mom had primary custody in those early years, I remember moving back and forth between my parents until I was eight years old. From kindergarten to fourth grade, I was at two different schools each year—half with Mom, half with Dad. My mom had her own issues and was prone to be abusive or absent. At one point, I told my dad that I wanted to live with him and never go back to my mom's. I was also scared of my stepdad. He abused us physically, mentally, and emotionally, and none of us felt safe living with him. I also thought it would be easier to get what I wanted at Dad's house. I moved in with my dad and stayed with him until I left at age sixteen, when my life got really screwed up.

Dad

Once I made the decision to live with my dad permanently, things were better. Even though I had to visit my mom regularly, the abuse almost stopped. However, the damage was already done. Every time I would come home from my mom's, my dad would have to lay with me to calm me down. He taught me deep breathing techniques, and I would go to sleep listening to "Jonathon Livingston Seagull" by Neil Diamond. This helped with the tension and stress, so much so that I still use those techniques today.

I was a broken, troubled child, and even though my dad saw it and sent me to counseling, the sessions didn't help at all. I would just lie to the counselors and tell them what they wanted to hear. I was afraid that if I shared what really happened at my mom's house, my sister, brother, and mother would all be punished for my honesty. I was afraid they would tell me I was wrong or that they would think I was crazy.

My dad and stepmom were very mellow in comparison to my mom. When I was younger and at my dad's, it was great. Life there seemed almost normal. My dad built us a huge wagon all six of us could easily fit in. We would pull that thing everywhere, or one of us would push the others up and down the street. That wagon was a great source for entertainment.

We had collies, rabbits, chickens, a mean rooster, and even a turtle. But even in a more stable home, all kinds of things happened. One memory that really stands out is when one of my sisters went into the rooster's cage and the rooster attacked her while the rest of us watched in horror. I can still see her running and screaming with the rooster flaring up behind. Finally, she escaped with some pretty good scratches.

I had a rabbit named Dingbat. That's what my dad would call me when I got a little flighty, walking into walls or doors. Back then, I attributed the dingbat descriptor to misbehaving or being crazy, but now I realize those flighty moments happened when I was in my ethereal world.

One day, my dad told me he killed my rabbit by accident; it had gotten out, and he had thought someone was in the backyard. That night, we ate rabbit for dinner. You can only imagine how sad I felt when we sat down to eat. One of my sisters thought making a point to tell me how tasty my rabbit was would help ... not! I'm sure there was some psychological damage done there. When I was sixteen years old, I found out the truth. We were so poor that we were almost out of food, and since I was the youngest, they thought I would get over the death faster. My dad killed Dingbat so we could eat that night.

Another memory is the time the city drained the water from all of the fire hydrants on our street, completely flooding it. So, the four of us girls, fully clothed, went body surfing and floated around up and down the street. It was great! My dad and stepmom just let us play in the water with no cares. We had so much fun.

During the short time we lived in La Quinta, California, we would lock ourselves in the house, and one of my sisters would tell stories and scare not only me and my other two sisters but herself, too. It was always nice knowing I had someone around. We didn't have to talk (which wasn't my style anyway), but there was a comfort level in not being alone.

As I laughingly remember these experiences, I realize how deeply joy and drama intertwined in my life. My dad and stepmom tried hard to make life fun for us. Through the highs and lows we all had (and still have), it was a relief to be able to go to their house and just be kids.

My two stepsisters came with their own set of issues. The older of the two and I shared a room because we were both organized, loud, and easily given to anger. The other two were more mellow and quiet, so they shared a room. My step sisters came from an abusive father. So much so, that he once threatened the older one's life so badly that the cops came to dispel that situation. We were a hodgepodge of major dysfunctionality, to say the least.

Along with my anger issues, I was not nice to my stepmom. I physically fought with her and tried her patience. On one hand, I thought she was evil, trying to take my dad away from me. But on the other hand, I was thankful she was there, I had two other two sisters to play with, and we could be a somewhat normal family. Looking back, she was a saint in my life, role-modeling love in the midst of chaos, all while dealing with her own issues.

Mom

Even though I was officially living with my dad, I had regular visits with my mom. I'm not sure how these visits were planned, because the court hadn't ordered them. I do know that when it was time to go see her, she was always late to pick me up; sometimes hours and hours would go by before she showed up. I would just be sitting there waiting with my bag. One time, she was over four hours late to pick me up, and when I got in the car, she told me she was late because she had to run errands. In my mind, I wondered why we couldn't have done those things together. I realize now that I felt I was not worthy of my mom's time or attention.

To this day, my mom is still late, and sometimes I still find myself annoyed by this behavior. In fact, it's a joke now, and people will even tell her that an event is happening two to three hours in advance so that she will be closer to being on time. This affected me so much that I do not like to be late anywhere. I used to get really anxious if I was running late, and if it's a really important meeting, I still get a little anxious. Breathe ... remember?

As I mentioned before, my stepdad (my mom's second husband) was abusive emotionally, mentally, and physically. He had a very bad temper and took it out on us. My older sister was always the caretaker for my brother and me. She was what I now call my own eldest child sometimes: M.J. (Mother Junior). With my stepdad's issues, I was always walking on eggshells at the house. I learned at a young age how to quickly gauge a situation to know what the energy was. That way, if I walked into a room and sensed it wasn't good, I would bolt. But sometimes, it happened so fast I couldn't get away and was subject to whatever.

One time, I made my step dad so mad that he held a knife to my throat. I was five years old and he told me it was because "I gave him the 'evil eye.'" Another time, he kicked my sister all the way down the hall while she was holding my brother (who was about six months old at the time) because he felt she was trying to be his mom and take his son away from him.

At my mom's, there were lots of parties, drugs, and alcohol. If people weren't at our house, we were over at someone else's house. My sister and I knew this wasn't the norm because when we went to our dad's, there was peace and calm and fun with our stepsisters.

One time, my sister and I tracked in mud right after my mom had vacuumed. She got so mad that she beat us with her shoe. Another time, she went to spank me, and I dropped to the floor like dead weight. She couldn't get me to roll over, so she went to go get something, and just then, my sister came up behind me and said, "Come on, let's go." We hightailed it out of there so fast. Fortunately, we lived on thirteen acres with orange groves on one side and grapevines on the other, so there was a lot of space to hide.

I recall starting to watch the movie *Mommy Dearest* and being unable to finish it because it was so close to home. I was physically uncomfortable and couldn't stop moving in my seat. I never did finish watching it, not even to this day. I didn't want to watch something that felt so close to my own personal experiences.

There were some good times with my mom, though. Around five or six years of age, she started raising collies. At one point, we had seventeen puppies, and guess who got to walk them? Me. There were sixteen fun ones, and one named Pumpkin who would sit and refuse to walk, so I would have to carry her everywhere. The puppies came and went, but the breeder dogs, Tara, Shana, and Bandit, stayed and were the best dogs ever. We also had a German Shepherd that mated with a Dalmatian, and the puppies all looked like German Shepherds except one. I loved going to dog shows with my mom. I used to walk away, go find a police officer, claim I was lost, and then listen to them say my name over the intercom. Again, no drama on my part!

My mom lived in a big, Spanish-style house with lots of acres and a large barn. We had a horse, a pony, a goat named Nanny, and rabbits. Nanny the goat and I didn't care for each other. Every time she saw me, she would buck me. Of course, I didn't have any problem retaliating either. Can you imagine a six-year-old girl and a goat fighting? She was a pretty big goat too. Maybe she knew instinctively that I had some real anger problems at that young age and needed someone to duke it out with. She *was* a Nanny goat, you know!

As I got older, there were fewer and fewer visits to my mom's until I turned thirteen and became more interested in the party lifestyle that was the norm at her house. When I was fourteen years old, my mom, her friends, and their kids all had a birthday party for me. It was the first time I got blackout drunk. I had tried smoking and had been helping myself to leftover drinks at her parties since I was ten years old, but this birthday party really launched my crazy teen persona. After that, I started bringing my friends to my mom's house to hang out and party. They thought it was the coolest place to go. No one watched us, we did what we wanted, and we could eat and drink whatever was available. It was all downhill from there.

Even though I was living with my dad and doing some of those things too, I was living it up and partying with my mom. It was so bad that I supplied the cocaine for my mom's retirement party when I was fifteen years old. The eighth, ninth, and tenth grades were my all-time worst. I was a messed up, angry kid, partying, selling drugs, and sleeping around. I never had a boyfriend, though. I had some small flings, but they didn't last long. I was too high to care. I smoked cloves until one day I started coughing up blood, but that didn't stop me from smoking other stuff. At my mom's, I hung out with her friends' kids who were also partiers. I also had a party clan while I was at my dad's. It didn't matter where I went; I had all the right people in all the right places. All the while, I was getting good grades, and my dad thought I was doing well. He had no idea what I was really doing. I lied to him continually and played the good girl when any questions arose.

Partying was the way I handled going to so many schools and having so many temporary friends and neighbors. I played out a lot of different roles. My true friends have been my sisters. If it weren't for them and our crazy survival tactics, I'm not sure where I would be today. We were all so different, and even though we were all working to stay sane with the insanity of our lives, we managed to have fun—and we still do.

Crazy Freedom

There were other people who played a significant role in my life, and I wonder where some of them are today. One friend who I had some crazy times with when we were freshmen in high school has passed. We used to take her dad's work car all the time to tool around town or get to and from school while he was traveling.

Here's a little background: My dad had been letting me steer the car while I was on his lap since I was around six years old. One time, he hurt his back while playing basketball and couldn't sit up in the car. He laid back while I sat on his lap and told him when to hit the gas and brake pedals. It took us about an hour to get home, but we made it.

Because of this, I was fearless, and so I always drove when we took my friend's dad's car. Then one day, bang—an accident. A driver in a truck and I were both backing out of spots at the same time, and I was hurrying because we were going to be late getting back to school. Our car was damaged and the truck wasn't, so we told the driver not to worry about it. When we got home, we pretended that we had just gotten home from school and found the car like that. My friend's mom called the cops and told them the pool guy must've done it. Somehow I knew that the cops knew we had done it. We didn't cave in though, and her mom believed us.

In my sophomore year, I partied hard and did all kinds of crazy things—lots of drinking and drugs, ditching school, parties, and taking a friend's Dad's sports car to Palm Springs (an hour and a half away) without asking. Thank goodness we didn't crash that one!

When I was sixteen years old, I moved from Southern California to Northern California to live with my ex-stepmom (my dad's second wife), her husband, and my two stepsisters. Living with them was great; one of my sisters was attending Berkeley, and I would go there to party with her and live the college life I would never have. I managed to live with my ex-stepmom for a year before leaving for

Greece a month before my eighteenth birthday, against everyone's wishes.

During that year, I graduated high school early from a continuation school, lived with a homeless man who had moved into my stepmom's house, attended and volunteered at workshops with Tony Robbins, walked across hot coals four different times with him, and worked two jobs most of the time.

When I came back from my trip to Greece, I moved in with my dad and his third wife because my ex-stepmom didn't agree with my decision to go to Greece by myself and was upset that I'd lied to her when I said my parents told me it was okay to go. Upon my return, she asked my dad to come get my stuff and pick me up from LAX. I didn't stay long with my dad before getting an apartment of my own with a roommate. That roommate didn't work out, so I got a new one. We met while we were in massage school, and she is one of my dearest friends to this day.

We were young, dramatic, and had fake IDs (I'd had multiple fake IDs since I was fourteen). As you can imagine, we went to the clubs and stayed out till morning. Even though we had fake IDs, neither one of us were big drinkers; I guess I had already done my fair share by then. We just wanted to dance, and dance we did. We even had one club ask us to come back every weekend—they let us in for free so we could get the place jumping. We didn't wait for the guys to ask; we would just get up and start dancing. And we all know how dancing works: The floor doesn't fill up till someone else gets up and starts. We were the "someone else."

When I completed my massage course, I went to work for a chiropractic office. Pretty quickly, I started dating one of the patients. This man was a bit older than me; my guess is that he was in his late twenties, maybe very early thirties. He was divorced and owned a home. I enjoyed seeing him, as he was very kind in all of our interactions. He wanted a stable, solid girlfriend, and I didn't know how to give him that. Toward the end of our short relationship, I had to be seen by an emergency physician for severe menstrual cramps. Upon arriving at the office, I learned that I was actually having a miscarriage. The doctor confirmed this news and immediately performed a D&C.

This was one of the most painful things I have ever experienced. I went home and told my roommate what had happened, but for some reason, I didn't tell the man I was dating. In hindsight, I realize that I didn't have the coping skills to share my pain or upset with him. I was afraid of what he might say or do. I didn't believe I deserved a loving, caring response, so I kept my suffering to myself. After a few short months, we went our separate ways, and he stopped going to the chiropractor. This was a sad time. Even now, when I think of the relationship, I feel sad. He was a very good person, and I really liked him.

Next I started dating my boss, the chiropractor. I know what you are thinking—big mistake, and you'd be right! He sensed my vulnerability and preyed on that. Thank goodness it didn't last long.

About this same time, my roommate was planning on moving, and my mom was getting ready to leave for Northern California. At the last minute, I spontaneously decided to go with her. This is one of the places in my life that I was divinely guided to make an immediate change.

My mom's plan was to live in a 17-foot trailer on the ranch grounds of a winery and be a chef. I said, "I'm coming with you." You know I had to have been

My mom and I in 1987

crazy to want to move from my city life to a town with only one stoplight where everyone knows everyone. My aunt (my mom's sister) and uncle lived there, and they got my mom the job at the winery. My mom had no formal training, but she has an amazing gift for cooking. (She didn't when we were growing up, though. She could bake amazing things, but when the dogs wouldn't even eat what we were having for dinner, there was a problem.) Once we'd settled in at the winery and ranch, I became a server by night, and worked in the winery by day.

This was the first time that I'd lived with my mom by myself, and it turned out to be an awesome experience. We shared so much with each other, admitting and accepting some things and overcoming others. We laughed and cried and really got to know one another. We were the female version of *City Slickers* before the movie even came out. Later, we found out that the ranch hands not only talked about us every morning with their coffee but also made a few bets about us too.

I have to tell this one story that I'm sure my Mom wouldn't want me to tell, but it's a must. This is only one of many little adventures we had. We used to walk all over the winery ranch (it *was* 23,000 acres), and one time, we took a different route than we'd taken before. There was a lot of livestock on the property, so we were used to going through gates or walking over those big metal slats in the roads to keep the livestock in. We were walking one of those roads, and I happened to notice that, in the distance, a very large group of cows had started walking towards us as soon as we went through the gate. By "at a distance," I mean about a mile or less away from us. We just kept walking but noticed that they were still headed in our direction. We know we are in cow country, so we figure, of course they see us and will stop coming because cows don't come to people like pets, right?

We kept walking, and then I noticed that they were now running towards us. We stopped to listen and realized that the cows are coming straight at us. We turned and high-tailed it back to the gate. Generally, my motto has been, and still is, that I don't run. Even if someone were after me, I would turn and say, "I'm not running, so do what you got to do." But those cows got the better of us, and I don't think we had ever run that fast. The sound of a herd of cows coming closer and closer behind me made me realize that all those scary movies I'd watched as a kid had a profound effect on me. I swore those cows were trying to trample me. They got within 10 feet of us before we made it to the gate and closed it. I had never seen so many cows stop as fast and abruptly as they did. As soon as we got to the other side of the gate with our lives, we both started laughing hard, so hard in fact, that my mom had to pee. Here we are, on this single road to nowhere, with nothing around us but the gate and 400 hundred cow eyes watching our every move. So she just had to pull those pants down and go. There was no hiding what you got to do.

Unfortunately for her, out in the country, there is a lot of standing water, and with standing water comes an unbelievable amount of mosquitoes. I do believe on that day, they saw their jackpot, and all of them went straight for it. All of a sudden, my mom starts slapping her bum while trying to pee, and what do I, the helpful daughter, do? I start laughing even harder than when we'd escaped with our lives from the depraved cows. It was so bad that I had to go and shoo them away just so she could get her pants up and we could leave. We walked back trying not to laugh, flailing our arms to keep the mosquitoes away, and her scratching like she was trying to remove her skin. What a sight to see, and thank goodness none of the ranch hands were around to see it (at least I think).

The next day, we nonchalantly inquired as to why cows would come running to humans for no apparent reason. Well, this just goes to show that city folk have a lot to learn because just as we feed house pets, so too the cows came running to be fed. They thought we were bringing dinner. While we ran for our lives, they were thinking dinner is here—ting, ting!

The Falsehood of Adulthood

Shortly after that, Mom and I moved off the ranch, with the trailer in tow, to my aunt and uncle's house in Middletown. Mom then moved away with the trailer, and I stayed with my aunt and uncle for about a month.

My mom was still in party mode and dating a much younger man who shared her love of cooking and alcohol consumption. Her boyfriend had an older roommate who looked like an old-time country music crooner. My mom asked me to go on a double date at the road house restaurant near where she was staying, and then back to their house. After too many drinks, the country crooner and I began a week-long sex and alcohol fling. It all came to an end when I overheard him tell my mom he wanted to marry me. I never went back after that. I didn't want to have sex with him in the first place; I just felt obligated to do so in exchange for human connection. I wanted to feel loved, but when he wanted to marry me, I bolted. There were several other guys that I was sleeping with around town, but I had no desire to have a boyfriend.

One day, the chiropractor and I reconnected by phone. He had called my dad, looking to talk with me. My dad had been pretty irritated about the relationship, but he told me about the phone call anyway. When I called the chiropractor back, he invited me to meet up with him and his family in the Berkeley Hills area. A part of me dreamed that this meetup would lead to the stable relationship I longed for, so I eagerly accepted the invitation.

I picked him up at the airport, and we drove together to his sister's house. I met his family with an awkward introduction and clear disapproval. Still, in my desire to have a connection, to be loved, I stayed with him that night. We had sex, as we'd done many times before, and I left the next day to go back to Middletown. I felt ashamed of myself for having sex with someone who I could tell had no intention of having a relationship with me, and I just wanted to go home. I had so desperately wanted this to be something different. I just wanted someone to love me. I wondered when this pattern of disconnect between my heart's desires and my actions would end.

When I found out that I was pregnant as a result of this meeting, I went numb. Or maybe I was already numb. I was clearly disassociated from my personal well-being, and in turn, disassociated from the idea that this was a child I was carrying in my womb. Instead, it felt like a situation that had to be resolved.

When I told my mom, she said, "You're not going to keep it, right?" Given my free spirit, you might think I'd rebel against her advice, but instead, my numbed-out response was to say, "Uh, no, I guess not." I moved in with one of my mom's friends in a different town, and I called the chiropractor to tell him I was pregnant and planned to have an abortion. I explained that I would pay for half if he would pay for half. He asked me, "Is it mine?" I assured him it was; I had not been with anyone else near or around my time with him. It took me three more calls requesting the money before he actually sent it.

An appointment was made, and I had an abortion. When I went to the clinic, they did an ultrasound to confirm the pregnancy. The clinic practitioner kept asking me if I wanted to do this; she said that it was possible I was carrying twins. They gave me a picture of the ultrasound to hold. I kept looking at it, and I knew I was only pregnant with one. They don't knock you out for the procedure; they just give you a vaginal anesthetic. The practitioner said, "I'm here to help you through this. Just hold my hand and keep looking at me." As the doctor started the procedure, I just wanted to close my eyes. The practitioner kept telling me, "Don't leave me; stay alert." She kept shaking me so I would stay awake, even though I so badly wanted to pass out. The procedure was brief, and I never found out whether there was one fetus or two. To this day, I know there was only one, but I wonder what their intent was in telling me there were two.

I stayed with Mom's friend for a short time and then moved back to my aunt and uncle's house. A few months later, in January 1989, I met the man who would become my husband. My aunt and uncle asked me to leave because I was staying overnight at this man's home pretty frequently, and they disagreed with my lifestyle choices. As a result, I quickly moved in with him, and together, we made a decision to move to Southern California that spring.

Sex, Drugs, and Violence

You already know my story includes molestation and sexual and physical violence. In one way, my story is similar to many others. I spent years trying to deny these things occurred in my life. Yet, my subconscious (and painfully un-self-aware) choices actually served as a constant reminder. It turns out that many people who are molested, raped, or abused share common life behaviors, including insecurity, promiscuity, and disassociation. I was first sexually assaulted at the age of two, and this impacted every decision I ever made around sex and drugs from that point on.

My older sister was my caretaker during the early years of my life. My first sex-related memory includes her. I remember being in my crib, lying on my back, with my arms spread out through the slats of my crib on both sides. Looking over, I could see my older sister in a corner, looking frightened. Looking up, I saw our male babysitter staring at me in a menacing way. I could see a different kind of look in his eyes, a "hurting another human being and getting pleasure out of it" type of look. He used his fingers to penetrate me vaginally and possibly anally. I remember it being very painful and forceful. My sister told my mom about her own molestation by this babysitter, and my mom called the cops. Since I was only two years old, I couldn't talk about nor express myself with regard to what happened to me, so no one knew about it.

While living at my mom's house when I was five, I suffered my first concussion. While riding a bike, I hit a moving car. My sister's friend, who lived next door, had switched bikes with me, and her bike had no brakes. She took off first down a long driveway, and even though she yelled something back to me, I didn't hear that she was trying to say the word "car." So I pedaled as fast as I could to catch up to her, and I rode straight into the moving car. I rolled over the hood of the car and ended up on the ground on the other side of it. I remember being out of it and the driver screaming. When I came to and opened my eyes, my mom and sister were there, and there was a man standing in the background. At first I thought it was my dad, which made no sense because we weren't at his house and he now lived forty-five minutes away. Later, I came to learn it was my deceased grandfather. This was my first of many concussions.

Around that same time period, I started having conversations with this grandfather. He actually came around quite a bit. I remember seeing him when the dog had puppies and when I was playing by myself in my room. I also began hearing other voices in my head at this time. The voices kind of sounded like background chatter, as though I was listening to adults talking around me. I was not afraid of the voices; I knew they were just people talking, not anything scary.

Since I was afraid to say anything about them, I didn't want to engage them in dialogue, even though the spirits made themselves known to many people who came to visit at the house. These spirits moved things, turned lights on and off, and made lots of loud noises. It was common for us and others to acknowledge there were ghosts in the house, although I believe I was the only one who could hear their chatter. Right after we moved out of that house, it was torn down, and human remains were found buried under the basement fireplace.

When I was young, I had so much anger that I used to beat up other kids in school. I mainly fought with boys until I realized that I preferred playing football or other sports instead of doing whatever the girls were doing. I was still pretty tough, though. None of the boys messed with me, or I would take them down.

In kindergarten, I had stolen some money. I didn't even know how much until the teacher asked me about it and told me I had taken eleven dollars; I thought it was two dollars. I was sent to the principal's office, and back then the principal could spank misbehaving students, so I got spanked twice that day—once at school and again at home.

While I was still in kindergarten, I pulled a boy's pants down (underwear included). I got the double-spanking again that day. When my stepfather found out what I'd done, he sent me to my room where

I cried—in his words— "uncontrollably." He called me downstairs and told me that if I didn't stop crying, he would "give me something to cry about even more." He then said that I gave him the "evil eye," held a knife to my throat, and said, "If you ever look at me like that again, I'll cut you." In that moment, I could feel anger and extreme hatred for this man rising up in me. Looking back, I know what he was doing was not good, but at the time, the hatred came from my believing that he was responsible for bringing this abuse into my life.

I was a loner. In order to survive, I learned to just go with the flow. Don't stir the pot; don't make anyone mad.

When I was in first grade, my sister and I were horsing around like we usually did. We decided it would be fun to play rocket. This game involved my sister lying on her back and lifting me with her knees, then launching me into the air with her feet. On that day, it felt like I wasn't going high enough, so we decided to have her launch me from the couch. It worked. I flew up high and the whiplash from the launch knocked me unconscious. I briefly woke up to the paramedics working on me, and then fell back unconscious. The paramedics advised my mom that I had a concussion and recommended that she take me to the doctor, who confirmed that it was a concussion and recommended rest. One of my mom's dear friends was a nurse who stayed with me that night in case I threw up in my sleep. Her friend was right—I did throw up in my sleep— and felt grateful to have her there to care for me. This was the second of eleven concussions (that I remember, could've been more) that I would suffer until the age of twenty-one.

The next molestation memory came to me very unexpectedly. My friend JennMarie suggested starting our own book club during our commute, and I told her I had the perfect book: *How We Love: Discover Your Love Style, Enhance Your Marriage* by Milan and Kay Yerkovich. I'd had it for at least a couple of years; it had been a gift from my mom. I get carsick pretty easily, so I did all the driving and she did all the reading, no matter whose car we were in. It's a really thought-provoking book, and both JennMarie and I resonated with the content.

Then we came to the part about identifying with one of the four main styles of how we love. About two-thirds into the book, I started to feel really upset because I couldn't decide on my style. JennMarie gave me her opinion on which one she thought I was, but it didn't help.

We were almost finished with the book when something happened that changed everything. My husband at the time and I went to IKEA to get some things we needed for the house, and on the way we discussed him watching porn on the internet. At the time, I was still fully practicing Christianity and held the belief that pornography was a sin, that he was cheating on me, and it was degrading to women. Today, I have a more compassionate understanding, but in that moment, I was really hurting. My husband's response to my hurt was to say, "It's not like I'm forcing you to do this."

For some reason, the floodgates opened, and I started sobbing uncontrollably. Somehow his tone of voice and choice of words instantly took me back thirty-six years to a specific day and time of my childhood. Scenes started flashing through my mind. I couldn't talk to my husband, even though he must have asked me fifty times what was going on. I was vividly remembering that I had been raped and sodomized when I was seven/eight years old. A couple who lived next door to my mom and stepdad did this while they were babysitting me. They never verbally threatened to hurt me or my family; I just remember that the man said something to convince me that I had wanted it. I believed him because I really felt like I had no rights to my own body, not yet aware that I had been forcefully molested five years earlier.

I believe this unexpected memory recall was actually a divine intervention. I was becoming more self-aware. The time of the year happened to be the same time of year as when the abuse occurred, it coincided with when my youngest child was just starting to have sex, and now my husband had said something in a very specific way. All of this created the perfect opportunity for total recall.

Maybe some of you are thinking, "How do you just suddenly remember something so horrible like that?" Let me tell you, I had the same thoughts at one time. I didn't believe in repressed memories. I remember watching a daytime talk show featuring two sisters who had both suppressed the memory of their father sexually abusing them. I remember saying to myself, "They're lying. They are just mad at their dad and want to get him in trouble." I truly did not believe that people, let alone kids, could just forget something like that. How could something so traumatic be stuffed away as if it never happened? I even remember feeling angry at those girls.

During my months of therapy, I came to realize the depth of chaos that had been occurring leading up to this molestation. In truth, I had suppressed this memory because I just couldn't handle facing any more trauma. I didn't want to see it.

Just before this molestation occurred, a kid who lived a few blocks away and I were the only two kids who got off at the same school bus stop. We had to walk about five blocks to where his street was, and then I would walk another two blocks to my house. As soon as the bus drove off, this kid would kick me and taunt me all the way to his house. I had been friends with him for a while, but it hurt him that I didn't like him the way he liked me, so he took his anger out by kicking and hitting me.

One day my first stepdad was home early and I didn't know it. I came in crying because of the pain and shame. He wanted to know why, and finally, I told him what was going on. After waiting for one of his friends to show up to help just in case the confrontation got out of hand, he practically dragged me to this kid's house. He knocked on the door, and the boy's mother answered with the boy standing behind her. My stepdad threatened her, the boy, and his father with serious harm if he ever did anything to me again. They moved away shortly after that.

I was so afraid of my stepdad that, no matter what type of mood he was in, I was too afraid to be myself, to talk, to have any fun, and so on. So, when I was sexually molested by the couple who was babysitting me, I remembered telling myself, "I will never tell anyone about this." I was afraid I would be punished for accusing my mom and stepdad's friends of such abuse.

What I learned in therapy is that it doesn't matter how many times the sexual activity happened. The one main memory I do have was the catalyst that kept me quiet for years. This couple had primed me prior to molesting me. I can remember them showing me pictures in magazines; some magazines showed people having sex with animals, or same-sex acts depicting men-on-men and women-on-women. That led from magazines to videos to role-playing.

Not a soul, not even my oldest sister who had protected me so many times before, ever knew about it. My mom said later that she thought these next-door neighbors were kind of weird, but they were also available to babysit me. These culprits took advantage of that situation.

When we got home from IKEA, I went straight to my room and locked myself in there for five days. At some point, I told my husband what had happened. I didn't elaborate on the details, so he didn't quite understand the severity of what I was going through. I called the Employee Assistance Program available through my work and set up a counseling session with someone who specialized in this type of abuse. I told my girls, all teenagers at the time, about it one at a time, around day two or three. Of course, they didn't know what to do with the information either.

I finally told my sister after about a week. I did not tell my mom or dad until months later after seeing the therapist. I was just so unsure of how anyone would take this. I didn't want either of my parents to feel guilty, or that there was something that they should have done or that they should have known. My mom's statement was sobering: "This sure explains a lot of your behavior." She also told me how sad she felt that this was a part of her child's life experiences.

Remembering something like this can change one's demeanor for some time. It changed my carpooling experience with JennMarie from that point forward. I was not the chipper, happy person people were used to for quite a while. People at work knew something was wrong, even though I always tried to smile and fake that everything was going well. Inside, I wanted to scream; I was mad at the abusers, and I was mad at myself for not telling anyone. Thank goodness I had an understanding boss and coworkers to help me through this!

The counseling was really helpful for me. My counselor was a licensed hypnotherapist and on my first visit she did a hypnotic treatment to help calm me down. I went to therapy for about four months and learned about the statistics with this kind of abuse and gained an understanding that I was a survivor, not a victim.

Back to life on the funny farm ...

Between the ages of seven and eleven, my life continued down a dysfunctional path, changing back and forth between parents, changing schools, and changing friends. I also experienced my first French kiss.

The summer following fifth grade was the start of a series of summer trips to Mexico with my sister, her best friend, and her best friend's mom. This was in 1980, so there were no cell phones, no internet, and minimal landline availability, not to mention we were camping on a beach. My parents had no idea what was happening in my life at the time. I could have been dead, and who knows how long it would've taken for them to get that message.

The first trip to Mexico was the shortest of all for me, only about three weeks. We traveled through all of Baja, California, going down toward San Felipe, and ended up on a beach south of Ensenada. This location became our go-to spot for all of the following summers.

That first year, a few additional people joined the trip. We spent a lot of time driving around in a VW bus and felt truly adventurous. One of the adults had picked up some white lightning. I quickly learned that moonshine is one of the most powerful alcoholic drinks you can drink. The adults talked about how you could die if you drank too much of it, and somehow, that made it that much more interesting. So, of course, one of the girls and I made our own red punch cocktails. We were scared enough not to use an overly large amount, but curious enough to begin the practice of numbing the pain. Alcohol, followed by drug consumption, would now become part of my normal dysfunction.

These years still contained some innocence and, simultaneously, increasing times of losing my child self, beginning with that first French kiss. I accelerated quickly from make-out sessions to feel-up sessions to finger-banging sessions, all during my tween years. To quote the Eagles, I was living "life in the fast lane."

Living so fast, you might think I would have had sex much sooner than I did. Actually, I was afraid that I couldn't go back once I went down the full intercourse path, so I waited a bit. Around the age of fourteen, I remember asking my dad if I could get on the pill. He asked me directly if I had had sex yet. On that day, I had not yet had sex, but shortly thereafter, I hooked up with a high school senior, and we tried to have sex.

We went to the same high school, and he could sense that I liked him. One day, he was turning a corner and I bumped into him. Just like in the movies, I dropped all of my books, and he helped me pick them up. He said, "Your name is Andrea, right?" I stood there awestruck that he knew my name, especially since he was a senior and I was a freshman. He then said, "I know that you like me." I replied, "I know," and then he said, "I'm a senior and you're a freshman, so I can't be seen with you." I again said, "I know." Still looking straight into my eyes, he said, "Do you want to meet after school?" Of course I said yes. We agreed upon a day where we could meet at my house without any interruptions.

I remember being so nervous before he got there. I knew he was coming over for a full-on sexual experience, and I had complete hesitation, even though I felt unbelievably attracted to him. When he came over, we went straight to my room and started with the usual make-out session. He had all the right moves. There was a lot of really great kissing, and our clothes just fell off. He was so caring. He asked what I liked and what I wanted. That was new for me. I went down on him and had two big realizations. First, using words sung by Robert Plant, he definitely had a "big log," and second, I felt inadequate. I really had no idea what to do. In all my sexual encounters up to that point, I had just been the recipient of whatever a boy wanted to do.

This time, I was really invested in a shared experience, different from any time before. When we got to the intercourse part, like a true, true gentleman, he asked, "Are you still okay with me doing this?" He knew this was my first time, and that was in part why he was so caring and attentive. I told him yes, but after he made three or four attempts to penetrate me, I told him I couldn't do it anymore. With a careless, emotionless attitude, I dismissed him from my house.

One very important side note: I was completely sober at this moment. Unlike so many of my other rendezvous, I had wanted to be present for this one.

I couldn't go through with it because there was something both familiar and unfamiliar in this sex act. I had such a strong emotional attraction to this boy, something previously unfamiliar. And yet, when he attempted penetration, I defaulted to being, in the words of Pink Floyd, "comfortably numb" because the amount of force required for his well-endowed unit to actually enter me took me back (without my conscious awareness) to the forced molestations.

After he left, I found myself thinking that I didn't know how to do certain things. So I went to the library and checked out books on the subject. My relationship with my dad was such that I could have asked him, but my dad had always taught us girls that any answer we needed could be found in books. After all, my dad was a librarian, and this was standard advice about anything and everything we needed to learn.

I read about foreplay, intercourse, orgasms, and body parts. Given the memory-pain associated with this first attempt at sexual intercourse, I now further disassociated and began seeking out even more numbing tools, through drugs and alcohol, to make sex palatable. I had also found a wealth of information about our pleasure sensors, but this was something that I would not fully enjoy until some thirty years later.

From this point forward, I no longer said no to sex. Dissociation would now become another part of my normal dysfunction. Through the next couple of years, there were too many boys, and even some men, to count.

While sleeping around during the partying days in the spring of my fifteenth year, not quite yet sixteen, I acquired venereal warts, a common and treatable STD. I found a book that told me what they were, but with my school schedule, I couldn't get to a clinic to get them treated right away. I used this STD as an opportunity to party but avoid having sex. This was kind of freeing in some ways, because it gave me permission to say no, where normally I felt obligated to put out.

A few weeks later, my sister and our group left for our annual vacation to Mexico. This would be our fourth and final year of traveling and partying together in that location. Most of the vacation was pretty standard stuff: beach camping, partying, and horseback riding. Late in the trip, a seventeen-year-old boy, relatively new to the group, invited us to party. He left to get some pot, and later my friend and I went to meet him at a nearby dance bar. We drank for a while, he took turns making out with each of us, and then he said the pot was back at a house.

At this point, my friend and I were so drunk that we were practically incoherent. In this drunken stupor, we easily followed him back to the house. Right when we got there, my friend sat on the couch, put her head back, and passed out. The boy led me into another part of the house, the bedroom, and locked the door. I remember walking into the room and wondering what room we were in because there were no lights on. By the time I realized it was a bedroom and thought, *Oh, no*, the door was already locked. He pushed me down on the bed, and I tried to crawl backward up the bed to get away as he was undressing himself. He forcefully pulled me back down and held both my arms down. He went straight in and raped me. As he was quickly about to finish, I remember thinking, *Fuck you. Now you're going to get venereal warts.*

Still lying there, I saw an older man standing near the bed. The boy held my arms down as the man approached me, and I started yelling and yelling for my friend. Thank goodness she heard me, kicked in the door, and got me out of there before the second guy could finish. As we left, I said to her, "Fuck 'em both. Now they'll both get venereal warts."

These stories all sound horrible, but this time in my life was also infused with a number of miracles. For instance, one time, my drug contact was not available, so I went to a Mexican drug-dealing house for a pickup. I knew I was being watched in a way that suggested danger was possible, yet somehow, I walked out of there without incident. I sensed there was a vibe in that room that smelled of something bad, and I had been spared. And then there was driving under the influence. I did that so often, statistics would suggest that something bad should have happened. Yet I never hurt myself or anyone else during that time. This too was a miracle. Countless more experiences of "being saved" have happened to me over and over.

I knew that if I continued down the partying path, I would either die or go to jail. I didn't want either, so I decided moving would help me break this cycle. I left for Northern California right after my sixteenth birthday. My ex-stepmom was willing to take me in and help me get my life straightened out. Well, you can take the girl out of the party, but you can't take the party out of the girl. My partying ways came with me, and I just added college stories and then some to my exploits.

While living with my ex-stepmom, I received a phone call from a complete stranger from Greece. I thought it was a wrong number, but he kept calling me back, day after day. One day, he invited me to come see him in Greece. He said he would pay for half my ticket and had a house for me to stay in. Since I had already completed all my schoolwork to graduate from high school, I was free to go. I went to the local travel agency, and using my money from working two jobs, I bought a ticket to Athens, Greece. I forged my mom and dad's signatures to get my passport, because it was still a month before my eighteenth birthday. My ex-stepmom did not like the idea, and she asked me if my parents were okay with me going. "Of course," I reassured her. Well, she wisely didn't believe me, and she summoned my mom and dad to assist her with talking me out of going.

The only thing I remember about meeting with the three of them (and some siblings too) was how stupid I thought they all were. Finally, I got fed up and turned to my mom and dad and said, "Don't you think it's a little late to want to be parents now?" and walked out. Later that week, my ex-stepmom took me to the San Francisco airport, and that was the last time I saw her for several years.

When I got to Greece, I had no idea what I was in for. Apparently, I had described myself to a tee, but the older gentleman who approached me was clearly not what he had described. The dark hair was about the only thing that would have been a match. I do believe that the words that formulated in my mind were, "Oh shit!" as we drove the five or six hours to Olympia with little or no talking. His broken English was good enough to smooth talk, and that's about it. Plus, I didn't really care to know anything about a man who was old enough to be my dad. My excuse was that I was jetlagged and tired.

I actually was jetlagged, because I slept for eighteen hours. I have never slept like that before or since. I think it was my body's way of saying, "I need a break." It reminds me of the movie "Forrest Gump," when Jenny sleeps for all those days because of the abuse we put our bodies through.

After the jetlag wore off, I was able to walk around the town and see some amazing ruins, artifacts, and buildings. I took lots of pictures, but on my way home, I had to individually put the film in the X-ray machine, and all the film was exposed—every single picture gone.

During the day, I went sightseeing. At night I went to the local tourist spot—part bar, part restaurant. It featured old Greek-style dancing, and I loved that part. The first night I went, I met up with a group of college kids from London on holiday, and we spent all night partying together. I went back to the house after I knew the "wrong number" man would have left for work. His grandma would tell me things in Greek (I'm sure it had to do with me staying out all night), then I would sleep, get up, and repeat the process.

One night, I hooked up with one of the dancers and stayed with him all night. The next night, the not-so-accommodating "wrong number" man decided that he wanted to have his way with me. When I refused, he slapped me across the face. I knew at that moment that I had to leave, even though I had nowhere to go.

I went back to the bar where there was a party going on. Feeling angry over being hit, I joined the party, and lo and behold, several of the dancers were there. I was served Ouzo for the first time, and I decided that even though I hate black licorice, I would just suck it up and join in to relieve the pain.

I don't fully remember what happened after that, but I woke up to find myself in the middle of the backseat of a car surrounded by guys. I could see we were driving down a single-lane dirt road. The car stopped, and two of the men pulled me out of the car onto the side of the road. The first man raped me, while the other guy waited his turn. Two other guys just sat in the car (one of which was the dancer I had consensual sex with previously). I kept thinking, *This is not good—they're going to leave me out here when they are done.*

Suddenly, in the distance, I saw car lights coming down the dirt road. This was another miracle. There was no reason for that car to come down that dirt road except to interfere with what was happening. The second guy stopped penetrating me, gathered himself, and started walking toward the car. The dancer I knew started yelling at the guy who'd had his way with me, and an argument ensued. Then the two outside the car grabbed me, threw me in the car, and drove off. Again, not knowing exactly what they were saying because they were all arguing in Greek, I knew it was about what they should do with me.

I'm not sure where I slept that night, but in the morning, I walked back to the "wrong number" man's house, gathered all my stuff, and paid the dancer to take me to Athens. His uncle in Athens had a phone I could use to call the United States. I never did get any money from the "wrong number" man for my ticket, but I didn't care. I was just glad to be out of there.

Since I had willingly slept with the dancer the first night I met him, part of my "payment" for the drive, in addition to the money, was a stop on the side of the road to service him. When I got to Athens, I called my dad and asked him if he could change my flight so I could come home earlier. I still had two more full weeks, but I wanted to go home. Plus, I had no place to stay. The dancer's uncle had a hotel, but it was full that night. It was a small place, with only five floors, so there weren't that many rooms.

My dad managed to change my flight, but my new departure date was only a few days earlier than originally scheduled. He did help me find a hotel for the night, though. I hailed a cab to go to my hotel, and supposedly, the cab driver couldn't find this hotel. He finally just pulled over and said this was good enough. I got out, having no idea where I was or where to go. I started walking with my suitcase in tow and, after a block or two, I noticed I was being followed.

I started looking for a hotel, any hotel, just to get somewhere safe. I noticed a small hotel down a very narrow street, and I walked through its doors just as the two men who had been following me were literally two steps behind me. This was another miracle.

The desk clerk greeted me and asked if I had a reservation. Noticing the guys on the other side of the door, he asked me where I was going, where I came from, why was I there, and so on. He looked outside again and told me that if I had not come to his hotel, I would have been abducted. In the core of my being, I knew that. I was so thankful to be safe. I had very little money to give him, but he gave me a room for the night. He asked me if I had anywhere else to go, and I told him I would call the uncle's hotel to see if they could accommodate me for the rest of my stay. He told me I should leave the area immediately.

I told myself that I wouldn't leave my room until I was ready to leave the hotel. I had no food, so to take my mind off my hunger pains, I read the only book I had brought with me. I don't know why I brought this particular book because it certainly would not have been my first pick, but I read that book all night and finished it before I left the hotel. It was Shirley MacLaine's *Out on a Limb*.

It turned out that the uncle's hotel had a room available for me until my flight home. The uncle allowed me to stay there even before my dad could wire money to him for the hotel fees. He was very generous; he gave me a room with a view of the Parthenon. The light show every evening there was spectacular, and I felt so grateful. He gave me tickets for some boat rides as well. One boat ride was a day trip to one of the isles. On the boat, I noticed some younger kids who were speaking English. I listened to them at a distance, and then ended up meeting one of them in line for the bathroom. She invited me over to their table, where I finally got to talk in complete sentences. We laughed and talked all the way to the island and back. I also hung out with them while we walked around the island. I hit it off with one of the girls right away. She asked me where I was staying and said she wanted to leave the hostel where she was staying and come stay at my hotel. When we got back to port, we got a cab to my hotel, where there was a room available for her too.

She was from Los Angeles and studying in Israel. Her dad had passed away the year before, and his wish had been for her to study abroad for a time so she could get to know her Hebrew roots. The next day, we rented a moped and explored the city like tourists. We didn't stop at any of the ruins, but we drove by the large ones. We did stop to walk around the Panathenaic Stadium. We wound up getting an unofficial tour of the locked sections from a young guy who worked there. It was amazing. The whole stadium is made of marble; every seat is a circular slab of marble. It is an energetic masterpiece, and I was in awe of it. I could feel the excitement and joy of all of the people who had taken part in past events. I felt like I was in the movie Ben Hur standing there. It was miraculous.

Later we went to the beach on our moped. We weren't brazen enough to go topless, let alone completely nude, which was very normal at that time at all the beaches in Greece. I would just lay back and close my eyes; I was not ready to see all that nudity around me. Looking back, I still hadn't realized how being molested kept me from accepting others, let alone myself. We also went to outdoor shopping spots—so many stores with the same stuff lined up for blocks.

Then we decided to go and stay on the island of Mykonos for a few days. We rented a moped there too and puttered all over that island. While we were there, we found an awesome spot to sun ourselves. It was secluded, so we decided to brave it and go topless. We were lying there enjoying the peace, then I started hearing voices in the distance. I looked around, but there was no one in sight. We heard even more voices. Looking around, we realized that a busload of tourists had stopped at the top of the hill above us, and they were happily taking pictures of the scenery, us included! We rolled over so fast and just started laughing.

A couple of days before we were scheduled to leave, my friend got sick. The uncle told me to go to a local spot to get her some special soup. I dutifully took on my aide role, went to the restaurant, and got her some soup. While I was there, I made friends with one of the guys who worked there. He invited me back later that night and I, of course, accepted his invitation. He took me to the top of the restaurant where we had some food, then sex, and then I left. I went back the next two nights to repeat the same scene. Even willingly, sex in Athens was as unfulfilling as all of my other encounters. I had the obligation pattern down, though.

When I got home, I only told one or two people what really happened there. I pretended the whole trip was great, especially with my family, and then I moved back in with my dad.

I was just weeks shy of my eighteenth birthday. I had been molested twice by two different neighborhood babysitters, and I had been raped two times, in two different countries, with two men in line to do the act. I had also thought many times of ending my life. These thoughts were a constant stream. I did not feel safe or that I belonged anywhere. I had moved twenty times before meeting my husband, and then an additional ten times after we met until our separation. Although we moved a lot, we did get to spend one nineteen-year-stretch in a single house with our children.

A New Beginning

If you remember, after meeting my husband, he and I moved to Southern California. My aunt and uncle had asked me to leave their place, and I moved in with him for a few months. We then made a plan together; I was going to attend airline school, and he was going to pursue work in the trucking industry. The school was in Southern California, so off we went. This was followed by four additional moves between Arizona and California before we eloped in February 1990 when I was twenty years old.

Our decision to marry was certainly hasty. We had two reasons: We wanted to save on our income tax payments, and a car salesman suggested that we get married to qualify for a vehicle loan. So, on February 16, two days after Valentine's Day, we drove to Las Vegas in the car we were trying to buy, and we eloped.

When we arrived, it was late at night and all the chapels were closed, even though they all advertised being open round-the-clock. That should have been a sign. Instead, we went to the Frontier Casino and started playing blackjack. Now, mind you, I was not yet twenty-one, but I did have a fake ID, so gamble we did. It was my first time playing blackjack, and I got blackjack after blackjack, so the table filled and a crowd formed. The casino kept the rum and Cokes coming faster than I could drink them, and I got very drunk.

We won enough money to rent a limo and be driven around town to get a marriage license, return to a now-open chapel, get hitched, and return to the casino. That night, I was my typical loud self. My new husband had attempted to shake the blind officiant's hand, but of course the officiant, was unable to see his hand and ignored it. At that point I said, "I'm the one who is drunk, but even I know he's blind!" Listening to the audio recording of the ceremony, it was impossible to understand a word I was saying. I guess this is pretty symbolic of a marriage decision that came about from a need for tax savings and a car loan.

There was a shift in my husband after we were officially married. In hindsight, he started treating me like property, and I think I felt I had a duty to be a good wife. Maybe I wanted to prove to everyone, myself included, that I could be "the good wife."

I applied this approach to parenthood also. As a parent, I worked so hard to give my children an idyllic childhood filled with stability and love—all the things that felt outside of me at the time. Now, when I look back, I see that I was holding on to what some call a false belief. I wanted to believe that everything was stable, that somehow this would make my children better and happier. I loved them with all of my heart and soul, yet I denied the truth of being my full, authentic self. And it turns out that even when we do all of the theoretically "right" stuff, our kids still have their own journeys. It's kind of interesting being in my own place of self-discovery as they too walk in theirs.

I got pregnant in December 1991. My husband was working for a large milk delivery company. The following spring, the Los Angeles riots started, and they were right in the center of his work route. They began on Wednesday, April 29, and he had Thursday and Friday off that week. When he went back to work on Saturday, he could only deliver to a few stores. All the others had been burned down in the riots. He took pictures to show me the damage. Viewing the pictures and watching it unfold on TV only caused my fear to grow. I knew he was right in the thick of things. Being pregnant, the fear of having a fatherless child further increased my anxiety. The following month, he was robbed at gunpoint, his personal items were stolen, and he was beaten. I remember adamantly thinking that we had to get out of there, and together, we decided to move back to Northern California.

My husband is five years older than me, and marrying so young had its advantages and disadvantages. In the beginning, we lived a newlywed life. Everything felt good, we were always happy, and it seemed like nothing could go wrong. We were drinking together regularly and partying with friends. I got pregnant when I was twenty-one years old.

I gave birth to my first daughter at twenty-two, my second daughter at twenty-three, and my third daughter at twenty-six. My body went from normal to pregnant to breastfeeding to pregnant to breastfeeding to "I can't stop feeling like I'm pregnant" to pregnant and back to breastfeeding in five years.

Three pregnancies in such a short amount of time took a toll on my body. I was in terrible pain after I stopped breastfeeding my youngest. I had nonstop bleeding, mood swings, cysts on my fallopian tubes, fluid buildup in my uterine lining, and hemorrhaging ovaries. It took a three-year battle with insurance companies before they would agree to give me a hysterectomy. I had a full hysterectomy when I was only twenty-nine years old. Ironically, my great grandmother, my grandmother, my mom, and others all had hysterectomies at the ages of twenty-nine or thirty.

Having three children so close together changed our dynamic from partying to parenting. During this time, I focused on motherhood. I wanted to be a good wife, and now I wanted to prove that I was a good mother too. For me, the need for alcohol and drugs was replaced by my kids needing me to show up as a mom. I now had diapers, bottles, and onesies coming out of my ears. I felt like I washed more onesies in a day than any other clothing in my life up to that point. I remember trying to put a diaper on my two-year-old and wondering why it didn't fit. After several frustrating attempts, I finally realized that I was trying to put a newborn diaper on my toddler. This was a common theme with clothes too.

I attempted to try and get back a sense of control by becoming super organized with drawers, clothes sizes, naps, names, and even family timing. Even though I tried my hardest to have some type of normalcy, this time of my life is still a blur. Trying to remember exactly what we were doing or where we were can really only be captured with dated photos. Even that is unreliable, because my two oldest looked so much alike in their early months that if the photo doesn't have a name, I still am not sure which child is which.

My husband and I were living a routine marriage. We weren't really a happy couple, but it was comfortable, and we both liked being comfortable. We really were predictable. The girls and I learned to walk on eggshells to not upset my husband, and he learned he could use his loud, domineering style to keep things the way he wanted. It wasn't right or wrong—it was just the way it was. He used to start most of his sentences with, "The problem is ..." and this perpetuated my need to overcompensate by making things happy and right. I was always trying to make things okay for a person who never felt like anything was ever okay.

When I first sat down to write this book, I skipped over this part because it's so hard to look at. My marriage of twenty-six years was difficult. From Vegas to the very last day, it was always merely a matter of convenience. My husband had an expectation that the wife should provide sex as needed. And while I was able to fulfill that when we were still partying, sobriety and the demands of parenting made it difficult for me to put out. I used our kids as an excuse to avoid this wifely duty whenever possible. We had frequent arguments about sex and finances. My husband would often tell me that he was "taking care of me" because he brought me to orgasm before or during intercourse prior to his release. Neither of us actually understood the level of trauma I had faced in that aspect of my life and how this played a significant role in my behavior toward him and his desire for sex. The more he pushed, the more I rejected. Still, wanting to be a good wife, I eventually learned to drink wine so I could sleep with my own husband.

We were really good at triggering each other in many ways. When I got sick, it reminded him of his own childhood struggles with an ill mother. He didn't want to be anywhere near the illness or the hospital; he wasn't even around when I had to have surgery. We both liked to have control over our circumstances. I focused my control tendencies on the kids, and he focused his on sex and money. His way of asserting control often included quite a bit of verbal abuse. The whole time we were married, it wasn't so much what he said as *how* he said things.

Whether his tone was strongly opinionated, mocking, or belligerent, it was always all about him and what he needed and wanted.

At the same time, I was working through my stuff too. Sometimes I would do things that remind me of my mom, like yelling at the kids. I would instantly judge myself as a terrible mom, which then would result in my needing to check out. This would cause me to go through the motions of parenting without actually locking anything into my memory. Instead, all I could hear was the blaming thoughts: "How could you do that?", "How could you say that?", and so on.

To our credit, we actually started counseling four times. We had a pattern, and it always started out good. We would begin to discuss with the therapist our goals for being there, agreeing that we desired a better marriage and wanted to work through our issues. My husband would take responsibility for his contribution to some of our challenges. We'd make it through two or three introductory sessions just talking, and then after a few more sessions, he wouldn't want to go back. The end always seemed to come when he was asked to talk about his early years. Counseling would stop, and we'd fall back into our old habits.

I used to tell my girls each time we were going somewhere that we were on an adventure because life is an adventure. The one thing my husband and I did well together was vacationing with the girls. For many years, we would go to Pismo Beach for Super Bowl weekend with some friends. We tried tent camping once, but one night, a skunk came to visit our camp and tried to get into our tent right where my oldest daughter was sleeping. She freaked out and slept in the Suburban the remainder of the trip, vowing to never tent-camp again (which she still hasn't done to this day). Next we got a trailer and went camping as much as we could as a family, and sometimes with friends.

The girls and I flew to Wisconsin for church camp four years in a row, and that was always fun because I got a break. My husband didn't come on these trips, so things felt easier and more relaxed. The camp did most of the heavy lifting with the girls, so they didn't need much from me during that week either.

I always made a big deal of my daughters' birthdays. That was their one special day to claim as their very own, and I wanted to make it big. I loved having the big birthday parties with lots of family and friends. Out of this came the balloon fairy, who would deliver balloons to their bedrooms in the middle of the night. They would wake up to a bouquet of balloons just for them. Once, when the girls were later in their teens, I thought they would be too old for that so I didn't do it that year. Oh, what a mistake that was! My oldest daughter's birthday is in September, my middle daughter's is in November, and my youngest daughter's birthday is in January. They all were so upset about the balloons that year that I vowed to continue getting bouquets of balloons as long as I could. Those bouquets became totally outlandish and crazy—Bob the Builder for one daughter's twentieth birthday, or Thomas the Train for another's, or Blue's Clues, Dora the Explorer, Elmo, and so on. It was over the top, but then again, I guess I have always been too.

One year, I heard a clear voice in my head. My oldest daughter was in second grade, and my middle daughter was in first grade. They went to public school, and I clearly heard a message telling me to pull them out. Without hesitation, I acted on this voice. I then homeschooled the girls for many years. Homeschooling was solely my decision, and it wasn't until much later that my husband confessed that he was mad at me for making that decision. I had not consulted with him, even though this was a huge decision, but that's how our marriage was. I always did what I thought best for the girls, and I simply disregarded the notion that some other decision might be best for the marriage or family. I never let him help make decisions for the family.

In this case, homeschooling ended up being a great experience for me and my girls. We were involved in so many groups, and because we were with a charter school, we were part of the public school system and received their guidance. We were able to take horseback riding lessons, drivers ed, and art classes. I remember my neighbor telling me that for being a homeschooled family, we weren't home very often. In hindsight, I now see that it was my way of creating a second childhood, one filled with love, adventure, guidance, and support. How we made it on one salary and some extra funds was quite a feat. It wasn't easy, but somehow, we made it work.

I found solace in going to church, and I was a faithful follower. I attended many of the studies and functions. I found great, supportive friends and an escape. Sometimes my husband would attend a function, but not often. I also loved taking the girls to other churches' functions so they could meet new people and experience new things. Church was a big part of my life for over seventeen years. My Christian fellowship helped keep our marriage together longer than maybe it should have, because I followed the church doctrine that God hates divorce.

All through the years, I was a truth seeker, even though I didn't know what to do with the teachings I didn't agree with or felt confused by. Sometimes I didn't even know why I didn't agree, but some things just didn't sit right with me. Now that I have learned more about my authentic self, I still have a love for the Bible, but now I view it with a different perspective, one that aligns with my spiritual knowing and path.

Having traveled to various church functions with the girls, I came to realize how much I treasured adult interactions. Simultaneously, my husband continued his rants about our finances. He used to check the receipts when I got back from a trip, and I began craving some financial independence. Around 2003 or 2004, both my sister and a friend got involved in separate real estate transactions that went poorly. In both cases, their loan officer was dishonest about notifications regarding fees and commissions. This prompted me to want to learn more about this industry, and I decided to get my real estate license. Once I obtained that, I went to work for a broker, planning to focus on being a loan officer. At that time, the multiple interest-only, creative loan options gave people the sense that they could afford a home, but it was easy to see that the proposed solutions might put a family in a predicament of possibly losing their house in two, three, five, or ten years when the amortization kicked in.

A woman I knew invited me to apply at her place of employment in the mortgage industry. I applied and got the job. It was as much fun for me as it was scary. My oldest opted to stay homeschooled since she only had two years left, while my two younger children went back to regular school. So it worked out for all of us.

I loved going back to work, and I liked knowing I would be contributing toward our finances. This should have helped us get out of debt, but instead, it allowed us to qualify for more credit, which then increased our debt. We bought more toys and more stuff, so we were right back living paycheck to paycheck.

That's the funny thing about our habits—they keep us exactly where we are. Whether I worked or didn't work, used drugs and alcohol or didn't, put out or didn't … ultimately, no matter what we tried, our marriage was conceived by two broken kids, and it stayed broken until the end.

Out on My Limb

It took me a while to actually realize how sick I was, but in April 2008, one day I got to the top of the stairs at work and had the hardest time breathing. Thank goodness one of my coworkers carried my bag to my desk, because I don't think I could've done even that. That coworker was very concerned, but I brushed him off and told him it was because I was working out and my body wasn't handling it very well. Well, he didn't believe me and went to get the big boss, who told me to go home and see a doctor. I cried; I didn't want to go. I had too much work to do. He didn't care about any of that, so I went home.

My doctor put me on disability immediately and said he wanted to run some blood tests. While waiting for a diagnosis, I had a dentist appointment. Sitting in the dentist's chair, I found myself feeling worse than what had become the norm. The dentist came in and noticed that I didn't look well, so he called my husband to come get me. We went straight across the street to the after-hours clinic. My oxygen level was dropping dramatically, which prompted them to call an ambulance. Off to the ER I went. I stayed there for four days, had many tests done, and in the end the diagnosis was that my boobs were too big and I needed a breast reduction. *Really? I have had these since I was eleven years old, and you think I can't breathe all of a sudden because of their size? I'm not that big!* I certainly wasn't going to spend my thirty-ninth birthday in the hospital, so I went home.

My regular doctor then sent me to a respiratory specialist. The pulmonologist ordered more tests and more bloodwork. He concluded that I had asthma. He gave me inhalers and medications, which did not work and only made my symptoms worse. For seven months, I fought to have some other diagnosis because I still felt sick, still wasn't getting better, and still couldn't breathe.

In early November 2008, I stopped going to all doctors because I was so frustrated with them and the system. One night, once again, I really couldn't breathe. I got out of bed and sat in the recliner. I felt as if I might pass out. I told myself that if it lasted for twenty more minutes, I would wake up my husband and have him drive me to the fire department around the corner because I knew the paramedics there could give me some oxygen. Well, guess what? I did that all night, every twenty minutes or so, telling myself the same thing over and over. Morning came and I was alive, so I figured I was fine. I didn't tell anyone about it and just tried to get through another day. This very same thing happened again in early December. Still, I didn't tell anyone about it; I just knew I was alive to live another day.

In both those experiences, I know I was in the process of leaving my body. At the time, I knew I was very close to death. Yet what happened to me did not look or sound like other near-death experiences I'd heard about. Instead, I simply felt as if I were floating outside of my body in the ether, only periodically checking back in with my physical body. This was such a strange experience; I did not want to tell a soul.

One day, my dad called and I told him that I still had no resolution and felt I was being given the runaround. He called my sister, who had become a general practitioner, and she was very upset to hear I was still sick. They all thought I was better and back to work. She made some calls, and within the week, I had appointments to see an infectious disease doctor, a rheumatologist, and another pulmonologist.

The second pulmonologist was my third appointment after the other two, and I was able to see him in the beginning of January 2009. It had now been nine months. As soon as I saw him, he said he was pretty sure he knew what it was. He wanted to do a bronchoscopy and scheduled it for the following week.

Now, my body is pretty resistant to drugs ending in "caine." Novocaine and Lidocaine don't do much for me. Marcaine, in heavy doses, still seems to work, but the others do not. Even with Lidocaine having been sprayed into the back of my throat and Versed in the oxygen, I should have been good to go. Nope. I was awake while the doctor stuck the tube down my throat and into my lungs. I was able to withstand him looking into one of my lungs, but when he got to the other, I started coughing and couldn't stop.

The respiratory therapist had advised me before the procedure that I might feel as though I couldn't breathe, but it would subside after a few minutes. I sat there for three minutes, as he had instructed me to do, but I knew something was wrong. I grabbed his arm and said, "Get me some oxygen!" I must have had a certain look in my eye, because, like a scene from a movie, he yelled at the techs to get something stat and yelled at another tech to turn the tank all the way up. In the meantime, I was slipping in and out of consciousness.

The next thing I remember was being wheeled over to the technician who reads ABG scores, a test that measures the arterial oxygen tension (PaO_2), carbon dioxide tension ($PaCO_2$), and acidity (pH). This vital information determines the pH of the blood and gas exchange. The test showed that I wasn't exchanging, and the technician practically yelled at me, "What's the matter with you, are you knocking on death's door?" I was close to death, for the third time in my life. Again, though, it was not my time to go. I remember thinking that there must be something still planned for me to do, because I was still alive.

My doctor scheduled surgery for the following week. This one went just fine. The really neat part of this surgery was that my doctor was testing out a new piece of machinery that went all the way to the ends of the bronchioles where the alveoli are and captured it on video. It was quite amazing to see. From this biopsy, he was able to determine that I had hypersensitivity pneumonitis (interstitial lung disease). My alveoli were scarring and preventing the exchange of oxygen to my blood.

He couldn't tell me what had caused this, but once he had a diagnosis, he was able to give me some medication to reduce the swelling. I was able to somewhat recover and get off the medication, but I still was not 100 percent. I was cleared to go back to work that October, but I couldn't quite muster up the energy to do that. Then, in January 2010, we had the air vents cleaned in our house and found the culprit: black mold, the kind you've heard about in the news that people were getting sick from. The guy who came to clean our vents said he had never seen it that bad ever. We got all those vents cleaned out, installed a new ultraviolet, antibacterial air purifier, and within two weeks, I was as good as new.

Being off work for those two years were some of the most trying times for me and for my family. My oldest daughter was still homeschooling, and she also was my primary caretaker. She had just gotten her learner's permit when I had to travel one and a half hours each way to the doctor, and I told her it was sink or swim. She went from practicing in suburbia to the streets of downtown Oakland. She was a trooper, and I am so thankful she was there to help me.

My illness was very hard on our marriage. My husband really didn't know how to handle the situation very well. We all did the best we could under the circumstances. For me, I believe this was the start of true change in my life and how I looked at things.

I began looking for a new job. It took me five months until, lo and behold, my old company had an opening. I was so excited to come back to work. I didn't even care what position I got, I just wanted to work. This is when JennMarie and I began carpooling.

We were both Christian. We believed that the Word of God was the absolute and final word, yet neither of us was going to church. I was studying the Bible with my daughters, and she and I would talk about Scripture or our beliefs. JennMarie had a car accident that left her knowing that God was with her and that her time was not up. That first year of carpooling was just about getting to know each other. Ultimately, this evolved further over the next three years into the spiritual self-awareness journey that I'm on today.

Carpooling gave us uninterrupted, devoted time to learn about ourselves through inspired writings, reflections, and attending workshops. This time allowed us to vent about work and release any negative thoughts or anxiety. More importantly, it allowed each of us the introspective space to go beyond our habits and begin looking for ways to apply everything we were learning. The more time I had to really understand myself, the more my perspective of the world shifted.

What was shifting? I could say my whole life was, but that's both all-encompassing and generic. What started shifting was my identity; it was a shift away from bad habits and behaviors and all my false beliefs about who I was. The shift was slow but steady. When I attended that very first class at the spiritual center, even though I wanted to walk out, I told myself, "No matter what, I'm going to stay and get rid of that old stuff I've been wearing and carrying." Something inside told me this was the place to learn. My heart was letting me know it was okay, but at the same time, my mind was saying, "Get the fuck out now before it's too late and you've been converted into some weird psychobabbler going on about how we are one with God!"

The day that really hit me was when I heard that we chose this life; we chose our parents. I thought, Who in the hell would ever choose to go through what I experienced? Are you kidding me? Why would anyone WANT to go through that? I wanted to bolt out of that door so fast, yet again, my heart was tugging at me to stay. Now I can say that all those books I read, the classes at the Spiritual Center for Positive Living (SCPL), and the other spiritual teachers I encountered are the reason for my transformation. And the reality is that we do choose. We choose to stay in our current life or lifestyle, or we choose to seek out our desire to find our authentic selves, no matter what.

At this time, in addition to being married to a man who was full of anger, I was having some challenges with my daughters too. My youngest was my most trying. She wanted the world handed to her on a silver platter and was incredibly stubborn, but she has a great heart.

She was a freshman in high school, while my oldest was attending a junior college and my middle daughter was getting ready to graduate high school. My middle daughter is very laid-back, but if you push her too far, she'll let you know. My oldest daughter is a lot like her father, but she has this loving and goofy, funny side to her. All three of my daughters look and act so differently. I tell people that I was with the milkman with my first, the beer man with my second, and the lumberjack with my third. Those were my husband's job titles at the time—it's funny, but they all fit accordingly. To put it mildly, we are all a little dramatic.

I have to interject a funny story about my oldest when she was six months old. She was in the other room, sitting up watching Barney. (See how you remember him? He gets stuck in your head and you can't get him out.) I was in the kitchen cooking dinner, when all of a sudden, I heard these shrill, high-pitched screams coming from her. I found her sitting with her legs open, her sippy cup between her legs. Her cup had fallen over and was dripping milk, period. That was it. I was standing there with my heart in my throat, and she was literally crying over spilt milk! At that moment, I thought, *What have I gotten myself into? I have a child crying over spilt milk!* Yet, being the child created by the milkman, it made perfect sense.

It was not easy. I understand how the caterpillar feels.

First, the egg is laid by the butterfly, which, in my case, was the memory recall and realizing that I needed change.

Second, there is the larva, which is the caterpillar. All the caterpillar does is eat and eat and eat. When they are born, they are extremely small, and as soon as they start eating, they start growing and expanding. As they grow, they outgrow their skin, which they will soon shed. That was me looking for answers. I was feasting on all the books, workshops, and classes, growing and expanding and shedding my old self.

Third is the pupa stage. Now, this stage is interesting because the caterpillar completely covers themselves, and inside the most exciting thing is happening: major transformation or metamorphosis. Everything changes; every limb, tissue and organ that makes up this caterpillar is overhauled. That was me accepting the things I cannot change about others and accepting myself for who I was. The covering was learning to really love myself, trust myself, and honor myself—fully embodying and receiving.

Finally, the butterfly emerges. A beautiful, colorful, free butterfly—that was me finally realizing who I was in this life and loving every minute of it. For the butterfly, moving through these stages can range from one month to a whole year.

When I look back at my life and everything I endured, I would not change it for anything. I realize that the purpose of all of it was to bring me to where I am today.

When I was living with my ex-stepmom, she and her husband went to a couple of Tony Robbins seminars, and then they wanted us girls to go. As a messed-up sixteen-year-old, the one thing I got out of it was the deep breathing technique he taught. He said to count as high as you can go inhaling, and do the same when you exhale. If you can count to ten, that was really good. Well, I could go to thirteen, so I was golden.

Later, Tony Robbins needed some volunteers for his upcoming seminars. For the next four seminars, I demonstrated how to walk across hot coals without burning your feet. The first time I did, I was scared and nervous. But I trusted what he was telling me and the mantra he taught me to say.

I knew Tony Robbins was special; he had such great energy. I wish that I had learned more from him back then. It could've sped things up for me, for sure. We were all honored to be invited to his wedding to Becky, his first wife. We drove a rented small RV to San Diego to attend. Roseanne Barr was his guest of honor (this was before she hit it big), and his mansion was so beautiful.

What came to light during counseling was that I had disassociated myself from life. Basically, I was numb to everything; I lacked feeling. There were certain overwhelming moments, of course. All three of my girls' births were so special, but I didn't have that feeling that parents talk about when they say they fell in love the first time they saw their child.

Since I eloped, I didn't have the experience of love and bliss at the wedding. In fact, I never went to prom, high school graduation, or college. My husband and I did renew our vows for our tenth anniversary and, for a fleeting moment, I felt some excitement and love. That's why birthdays were so important to me because I wanted the girls to have these exhilarating days of it being all about them, to feel special and have great memories of that day.

As I continued the metamorphosis of my life, my husband and I separated and eventually divorced. My girls understood, but at the same time, it was painful for us all. We had lived in our house for nineteen years. Our daughters grew up there, with painful, exciting, sad, and wonderful experiences forever associated with that house.

Learning to purge stuff is one of the most exhilarating things to do. I realized that in order to move on, I just had to get rid of stuff. I had the urge to purge. Making the decision to move into a fifth-wheel trailer magnified what I really needed and what I didn't. I held on to some things I really liked, but for the most part, I got rid of an entire house. If you ever get the desire to get rid of stuff, do it. It's so freeing. We collect so much stuff. I had to shift that stuff's energy out and away. Years of stuff leaves a mark on you. Even if it's just a small section, purge and get rid of those things that no longer have relevance to your life. Keep the memories; lose the stuff.

Things began to shift in a big way. At first, it seemed nothing was really happening, but I soon came to realize that there are surface changes, and then there are deep changes. When I went to my first workshop, Personal Evolution, there was a deep change. In one of the meditations, I had this vision of a tar pit in front of me. There was a dead tree next to it, and as I was looking at the pit, I realized someone was in it. I broke a branch off and used it to pull in the person. I dragged him to the shore and saw that his hands and feet were bound, and there was tape over his mouth. I cut him loose and removed the tape. As I looked into his eyes, I saw how thankful he was. I cleaned off the tar, and when we were finished, the tar pit had been transformed into a sandy pit, and next, grass began to grow over it. The tree bloomed into a beautiful cherry blossom tree. I knew that this was who I thought I was: bound and covered in sticky, yucky tar. I hadn't been able to escape my past in the tar pit, but now I was free. I was clean and safe from harm.

The next significant shift came when I became aware of the first time I was molested at age two. From that revelation came the understanding that, because I was not talking at that time and no one knew I had been assaulted, I couldn't use my voice. What a revelation to know that even at such an early age, we can learn these vices to prevent us from being our true selves. I couldn't talk then, so I was not going to talk about my true feelings with anyone later in life either.

One of the other workshops was on communication. I liked the meditation coaching workshop, but this one, um, not so much. Though I did play full out, I also used some of my disassociating skills to pretend it was not really me who was talking. Finally, on a couple of experientials, I did let myself be fully in the situation. I needed to feel, experience, and say those things with my own voice.

Surface changes occurred when I began to recognize that I did or didn't like something and spoke up. I could honor myself in this way, which is really loving yourself. I also began saying affirmations; they really do work. Louise Hay tapped into something all those years ago when she was made aware of how impactful positive affirmations are to bring about personal change. I didn't have a clue what it meant to love someone, especially myself. We can't love others when we don't know how to love ourselves.

The most impactful practice for me was looking into each eye and telling myself that I loved me. One day, I was frustrated with myself because I knew I was just saying the words. We can say the words over and over, but I wanted more. I didn't know what the "more" was, but I knew I wasn't giving it to myself. So I stood there for what seemed like a very long time and kept saying, "I love myself" over and over, looking into each eye. Then *bam!* It hit me and something shifted. I felt it in the deepest part of my gut. It was a knowing, and a solid foundation was laid right then. I *knew* that I had changed my neuropathway and my DNA. This time felt different, and when I said it to myself again later, it felt different then too. Something had definitely shifted.

Loving ourselves means honoring and trusting ourselves. Trusting ourselves means loving and honoring ourselves. And yes, honoring ourselves means loving and trusting ourselves. These three are intertwined. One can't happen without the others following suit.

And once you know what you know, you can't un-know it.

Crazy Self Love

People often think I was born with an abundance of self-acceptance. They mistakenly assume that my openness equals a mark of confidence. I find that when I share my story, it makes others feel safe to do the same. My invincible truth is that I work at self-acceptance. In my human form, self-acceptance is a vital part of this journey. It is a walk that I am proud to take. The process of writing this book has been a part of that work. Making peace with my childhood truths and rediscovering my spiritual connectedness has led me to a whole new level of self-acceptance.

Realizing that I am both my past and my present brings me to an authentic version of my future self. The Bible says that God is the past, present, and future. We are too. I grew up a wild, rebellious, and defiant girl. I lost that girl somewhere in adulthood, and it is only now that I'm beginning to see how beautiful and amazing she really is.

The story of Judas in the Bible is extraordinary. The traditional Christian interpretation of Judas is based on the premise that he is the ultimate traitor. He sold out Jesus for thirty pieces of silver. There is actually another side to this tale, however. A second-century Gnostic Gospel, discovered in 2006 by the National Geographic Society, asserts that Jesus asked Judas if he loved him enough to help him ascend to heaven by committing betrayal. Modern day teachers refer to this type of commitment as a soul contract. I believe in soul contracts, and I know that every step in my journey has been in service of my soul's growth.

In the case of Judas, the elders knew where to find Jesus. They still gave the money to Judas to validate that they had found the right person. Judas's role was to fulfill a prophecy, and he fulfilled that commitment as promised. Within days of Jesus's ascension, Judas killed himself. Why? Because he remembered his soul contract, knew that it was fulfilled, and he was ready to move on for his own soul's evolution. You see, as long as we fulfill the contract, our soul evolves;

we prepare for even more bliss in our human form and beyond. If we ignore the contract or try to skip out on it, we will create similar situations again and again until it is complete.

Looking back at the dangerous events I endured—molestations, rapes, verbal abuses—none of them resulted in my demise. Early on, I had contemplated suicide, but I really knew it was not for me. The precarious situations that arose over the years simply pushed me closer and closer to my spiritual truth. Now, with the benefit of hindsight, would I have liked to have reached this understanding a little sooner? Absolutely! And, at the same time, I would not change a thing.

We can all be in this place with Judas in the blink of an eye by constantly remembering that everything is happening for a reason, and that reason is here to support us. This is true for the actions we do to others, as well as the actions done to us. Years ago, when I prayed the prayer of salvation, I turned to the two ladies there and said, "I just want to know the truth." At the time, I thought I wanted to know the truth in reference to the Bible and God. What I really wanted was to know the truth about myself. I've since discovered that truth is everywhere. I didn't need to learn the truth—I needed to learn how to step into it and live it all the time. To remember my truth.

When I was a Christian, I tried to fit in. I tried to be the good follower. I wanted to believe that I was obedient to the Word of God. I had many wonderful experiences with my church community, but I was not truly being myself. I was told that it was not appropriate to be a wild child in the church; I was a sinner who needed to be saved. Saved from what? Myself, the world, or my wild child ways? All of the above, according to what I was taught. If I wasn't saved from all that, hell was where I'd go. I hid myself away and pretended to be saved. It turns out, though, that in a way they were right, because living with my true self stuffed away *was* hell—and being saved by living in my truth really *is* heaven.

To think that we need to be forgiven for everything that has happened in our past in order to go to heaven, is living a life of judgment. I am learning that heaven is available to each of us in the here and now. Today, this moment, is our heaven or hell; we choose. The beautiful part is that I still love Scripture and quote it often. Jesus has come to me in my meditations. I still love to listen to Christian music. Because this is so much a part of me, you can imagine the grief I experienced when I decided to leave the Christian community that had provided love and support for many years. I had one friend in particular who had been integral in my daily life. We shared so much and had so much fun together. When I left the church, unfortunately, it included leaving this friend, who has stayed faithful to what she still feels is truest for her life.

Part of my awakening process is recognizing that even when things have served me well in the past, it does not mean they will be a part of my future. Losing a community and a good friend was not easy, but it was necessary for me to explore what was most true for my future.

When I reignited my spiritual path, I began attending classes and workshops. I received numerous spiritual certifications and mentorship opportunities. I was seeking guidance, clarity, and answers that contradicted what I'd previously learned. At one point, a friend asked me why I was signing up for so much stuff. I told her it was because I was getting something different from each one. No single teacher or school of thought offered everything I was seeking. I still found comfort in attending the Sunday service with JennMarie at the new spiritual center. The routines and predictability of the center made it easier for me to begin living authentically. And yet I realize now that I really only traded one organized religion for another. Even there, I was still looking to discover how to be a good follower. I wanted somebody to tell me the right way to live Christ's truth.

I loved the center I was attending because it incorporated many religions (Christianity included) into its teachings. I loved the people that went there too. The center had great energy, and the church experience so resonates with me, from the music and messages to the interactions. I liked it so much that I found a variety of volunteer opportunities to further the family feeling that came from this spirit-filled community.

During this time, I launched a side business as a psychic medium, and it started flourishing. Slowly my attendance at the spiritual center began to diminish. The more I engaged in the work of spiritual channeling, the more time I needed for self-reflection, meditation, and intrinsic guidance. I began to prefer to be in my own environment for meditations and, as a result, the messages became stronger. I learned to be more deliberate in my practice of connecting with my spiritual guides, receiving my own information and guidance.

Now that I was divorced and living on my own, simultaneously another side of me resonated amazingly well with my new neighbors. The wild child was being reawakened! I was riding Harley Davidson bikes and partying at campfires. That lifestyle is what I had always known growing up. It felt comfortable, and I felt accepted ... sort of. You see, I was still living two lives: my neighborhood life and my spiritual life. A few people knew of both, but most only saw one side of me. I didn't even tell my neighbors about my mediumship work until I could no longer hide it.

So how would all these experiences come together? Who am I? I had a Christian self, versus a spiritual self, versus a wild child self. I am all of these, and I knew it was time to fully accept all of these truths into one integrated version of myself.

Jesus and Buddha were not compelled to adapt to the environment around them, the way I had been doing for too many years. They are spiritual examples of being true to oneself in every situation, with every interaction, all the time. I was ready for this to be true in my life as well. Up to that point, I could be a part of myself in any situation, but I wasn't my full authentic self in all situations.

It was time to be myself and love that I am this "crazy girl." Most of my life, I had thought that being judged as being crazy came from family, church groups, or society at large. But my spiritual journey taught me that judgment only comes from one place: inside of us.

I was ready to overcome self-judgment.

Conclusion

Sometimes, when I speak, I can appear somewhat matter-of-fact about events that others would experience with significantly more emotion. Please know that I honor each person's journey. My matter-of-fact style does not discount the significance of the events in my life; it just suggests that there is another side of the story—a strength, a resiliency, a divine guidance that has served me. This is my attempt to capture the pain and the humor, the chaos and the kindness, the anger and the love. All of these are available for the taking, and I prefer to live in a place of humor, kindness, and love, even after walking through pain, chaos, and anger.

As a child, I used anger to overcome fear. As a teenager, I used drugs to suppress feelings. As an adult, I used work to avoid my insecurities, and I used the role of wife and mother as an excuse to not face the truth of who I was and what I wanted.

In searching for, and finding, my authentic self, I started down an entirely different path for my life. So many doors have now opened, doors I couldn't have even dreamed about with my old perspective.

Overcoming fear is a moment-by-moment experience for me. Learning to replace fear with love felt so foreign at first. But little bit by little bit, it became fun and exciting. It feels so good that I never want it to end. When the Bible says that love covers a multitude of sins, it's really true. The sin is fear. When we love ourselves, we allow everyone else to be on their own journey, and we love them for it. We don't know what the homeless person's journey or life lesson is, and to judge or think that we are responsible to change that for them is a misunderstanding. We just need to love them for who they are right now.

I have chosen to have an expansive awareness of the multidimensional realm around me and to give it back to those around me for the good and healing of others. Instead of allowing traditional corporate work to keep me trapped, I trusted myself and the Universe and have become an entrepreneur.

I have gone from being at home most of the time to traveling to multiple states and three countries in less than a year. I have explored my sensuality to a degree that I didn't know was possible.

At every group and one-on-one session, I learn something new that Spirit is revealing, sharing, or allowing me to explore in further detail.

Most of all, I have had more miracles, magic, and fun since discovering the truth of who I am.

There are so many other stories I haven't shared in this book. And yes, there are many other stories from people that are far worse than what I have experienced. My story is one about finding out who I really am. Yes, I overcame. Yes, I survived. Yes, I kept pursuing a good life. But that's not all of who I was. I am not just a survivor or an overcomer—I am a thriver. I thrive. I am genuinely filled with love. Every day, I wake up so thankful, loving this life I am living.

I love me. I enjoy me.

The takeaway in writing this section of the book, and the vulnerability that I want to share with you, is that we can get to a place where we recognize and accept our past and all our experiences as being here for us as part of our soul's growth. There is no shame, no embarrassment … only love.

What do we make of it all? Do we want to make it hard, difficult, and frustrating, or do we want it to be a free-flowing life of love and gratitude? We get to choose.

It might seem as though it would be easy to perceive my life experiences as totally wrong and terrible, but it is actually much easier to look at them as part of a healing journey that has left me feeling totally free.

We all have stories that remain unwritten. We each have our own interpretation of our experiences. This is my interpretation of my life up to this point. Going forward, I will share my interpretation of becoming spiritually awakened and learning to be in a state of love and freedom 100 percent of the time.

PART TWO: My Invincible Awakening

Introduction

Since conceptualizing this book, my life has radically changed and gets more amazing every day. In this section, you'll learn about some of the techniques and tools I have used to become more fully awakened. However, I am guided to tell you that there really is only one thing you must do to live an awakened life, and that is to love. Love yourself, love every choice you make, love every experience you have. Just love.

The year is 2016. I am in the studio waiting for my first television appearance and reflecting back on how this manifested so quickly. Just one year prior, I couldn't have imagined being on television, plus on top of that, talking about myself and my purpose as a Spiritual Alchemist. Up to that point, my life had been filled with chaos, and now that chaos was being replaced with magical synchronicity.

In Book Two, I'll share with you the circumstances and life events that supported this fantastic path of spiritual growth. I am imagining that you, the reader, have joined me because you too are seeking. I spent years exploring different schools of thought and pursuing certifications and mentors to support my spiritual growth. Even after having experiences with the Bible, archangels, spirit guides, and God, I still wanted to know what was true for me. It had to make sense for me. How could I be happy with something that is senseless? I was seeking clarity between the experiences I was having and the information that was available. Come along with me as I share my interpretation of the wisdom gained through my life experiences that brought clarity. I hope it makes you as happy as it makes me.

Getting From Here to There

Talking about my marriage and divorce is pretty straightforward. I actually knew early on in the marriage that I didn't want to stay married to my husband, and I told myself I would just stay with him until the kids were grown and out of the house. Life was not easy. In searching for myself and what I liked and wanted, I realized that my husband and I did not have much in common. When I finally decided that I couldn't play pretend with myself anymore, we separated. Some months went by, and I was guided to ask him to come back into the house. I knew it was not to reconcile, although I didn't exactly state that to him. For reasons that were unclear to me at the time, he moved back in for about six months. But after we celebrated our twenty-fifth wedding anniversary, I again decided that I couldn't live a life as a chameleon; I needed to show my true colors. Our divorce was final the following year.

I can't say that there was just one thing that led up to this point, and at the same time, I can say it was a marriage of living in denial, chaos, shame, and guilt. There were conveniences and expectations. Being married was a big part of my journey, though, and for that I am very grateful.

There was just one thing motivating me to live my life for me: getting to know myself so I could learn to love that person for who she really is. I wanted *that* more than anything. It turned out to be the easiest, freeing, and most exciting thing I have ever done, and my life is so different than what it was just over five years ago. My determination and strong will led me on the most expansive, growing journey, and I could barely keep up with all the exciting things that happened.

As I mentioned earlier, I had a corporate life; my other life consisted of sessions with groups or individuals. After my husband and I separated the second time, I lived in my fifth-wheel trailer and was free to do whatever I wanted. I loved my corporate job—I loved the people and the familiarity of a routine, yet also the "not knowing what every day would hold" vibe. In the beginning I worked five days in corporate and had sessions with clients every night (sometimes on the weekends too). It was a lot to handle. I was also traveling for work quite a bit which helped me to have time for getting away from all the stress of working two jobs and family drama. I felt really good that I was booked three months out.

I don't remember exactly what was said in the interview (which is no surprise as I don't remember any of my sessions), but I remember stating: "Well, my work doesn't know it yet, but I will be quitting soon." And I thought, *At this moment, this is recorded and will be out there for anyone to hear.* And guess who heard it? The Universe, Source, God. And it said yes. Two weeks later, I was given the pink slip. I had two months to square away my duties.

Working allowed me the benefit of attending classes, seeing spiritual teachers in person, and providing for myself. I knew I could still do those things, but HOW? My employer offered me the option to me stay by transferring to a different department, and yet I knew it was time to go. If I really wanted to help people, I knew I had to go for it.

In 2016, my divorce became final, I went to Brazil by myself, my oldest daughter got married, I got laid off, and I was free to be me.

My comforting, routine lifestyle was now gone. My life has drastically changed from married to divorced; gainfully employed with benefits to self-employed; and having excellent credit to having to file for bankruptcy.

Manifesting for Prosperity

Manifesting is a word frequently used by spiritual seekers. Sometimes it's used synonymously with prosperity. A common belief is that manifesting and prosperity are the same thing. Actually, though, they are two separate concepts that sometimes intertwine. Prosperity is a word used to describe success, wealth, and affluence. Manifesting is quite different—it is the process we use to bring thoughts to life. Human beings are manifesting machines. We manifest all day, every day. All those clichés about negativity feeding negativity, reaping what you sow, and thoughts being things exist for a reason: they are all true. We are constantly bringing forth whatever it is we are thinking.

Maybe you've heard stories about lottery winners who end up bankrupt just a few years after their big win. According to a study completed by the National Endowment for Financial Education, 70 percent of lottery winners file bankruptcy within five years of their big win. The research suggests that people get on a money high and think they're unstoppable. Interestingly, from a spiritual perspective, we are never unstoppable. So what is really happening when someone manifests what they've always wanted, and then loses it just a short time later?

I came to learn about manifestation when my dad and second stepmom began creating and posting vision boards. The boards contained pictures and words of things they wanted to attain. At the time, I thought very little about it. Looking back, I realize that I didn't feel worthy or deserving enough to want anything, so the vision board practice really didn't matter. Years later, that changed when I attended my first Tony Robbins event. This opened the door for me to volunteer in Tony's seminars four more times.

I walked across coals four times, as I mentioned before, and on the last one I burned my pinky toe on my right foot. This happened because I had lost my focus. We had been instructed to repeat a mantra to help focus our energy for moving across the coals without getting burned.

Three times in a row, I had successfully crossed the coals. On the fourth and final time, I momentarily got distracted from the mantra. I remember thinking, "This is my fourth time doing this." That thought was enough of a distraction to burn my pinky toe. Manifesting is just like this; we must learn to be diligent about our thoughts.

Even with the Tony Robbins training, I still struggled to receive the message that we could truly instantly manifest anything in our lives. I continued to feel unworthy, and I let the opportunity to pursue these teachings in more depth just drop away.

I had always believed manifestation to be about the successful attainment of stuff (prosperity). Today, I look at manifesting and prosperity much differently. If you search the internet for the word manifest, you will find this definition: "to be clear or obvious to the eye or mind." For me, manifesting is about focus and worthiness. The words "clear of mind" help me understand that to manifest something, we must have clarity of thought. Just like the mantra for the hot coal walk, disciplined thought is essential.

The funny thing is that you already have disciplined thought, whether you realize it or not. Your thoughts may be positive or negative, or like most folks, a combination of both. Look around your environment right now. What do you see? Everything you see is evidence of your manifestation powers. Do you like what you see? Great! Create more of it by expressing gratitude, appreciation, and compassion.

There were times when I looked around and didn't like what I saw. That's part of the reason I moved so much during my youth. Looking back, I realize that I rarely defined what I wanted, so my life stayed chaotic; that was the only thing I really knew. Chaos was my comfort zone. I was good at manifesting situations of constant chaos.

When I became a Christian, the newfound religion ushered in guidelines for me to follow on how to be a dutiful wife and mother. With these clear guidelines, I then manifested the life experiences that matched what was expected. That pretty much consumed twenty years of my life.

Learning how to consciously manifest came during a time of experimentation for me. I sought out so many spiritual teachers because I was looking for guidance on creating my best life. When I was actively seeking, I was striving to manifest things that would benefit my family. Ultimately, I came to understand that it is not in our best interest to look outside ourselves for what to believe. Nor we can manifest on another's behalf. Each of us learn and manifest what we individually need, and those needs are evolving all the time.

In my awakened state, my world has become vastly bigger as I expand my horizons across the globe. Simply by tuning into the larger world, new opportunities for travel have come up for me again and again. Within a short period of time, I traveled to Brazil; Oklahoma; the Grand Canyon; Sedona, AZ; Las Vegas and Carson City, NV; Florida; all over California; Italy; Croatia; Montana; Alabama; and Nashville. In some instances, I was invited to do my work in some of the cities, while other travels were purely for pleasure.

It's powerful to realize that all this manifested when my perspective switched from maintaining the status quo to being totally free. This is where the distinction between prosperity and manifesting becomes important. Just because you manifest prosperity, this may not necessarily get you closer to what you truly desire. I had to manifest freedom first; it was vital for my spiritual growth to live freely during this time. Freedom is essential for my sense of joy. What is essential for you? Now is the time to make it manifest.

The key to manifestation is simply understanding that it is happening all the time, whether you are conscious of it or not. Manifestation occurs while you are numbed out just as easily as when you are fully awakened. My goal is for you to manifest consciously so your life can be filled with all that brings you joy.

Discovering Rituals

Rituals have always been an important part of my life. My journey of awakening has led me to see the value of rituals more clearly and allowed them to be significantly more fulfilling. When you think of rituals, you may think of religion. While rituals are indeed commonly integrated into religious activities such as worship and ceremonies, the information I am sharing here is not focused on religious practices. Instead, I define rituals as personal actions that involve self-care and repetition for awakening one's spiritual connection.

When I was married, I had many habitual rituals that afforded me the opportunity to get things done fairly effortlessly. Some examples were always getting up before the kids to pray and read the Bible; making sure we had fantastic holidays and birthday celebrations; and homeschooling routines. Prayer, celebrations, and routines were rituals that kept me sane and relatively happy while raising three girls.

Rituals and habits are easily confused with one another. Habits are things we do mindlessly; we don't have to be present for them as they just happen automatically after weeks, months or years of repetition. My rituals became habits that helped our family be comfortable and brought order to my chaotic life. Ultimately, I came to learn that my habits were formed by my deep longing for structure and order. Interestingly, you might think that as I moved into a free-flowing, magical spiritual ride, I would dump anything and everything habitual. Actually, I didn't.

When I let go of the idea that the rituals had to create order, and instead embraced how rituals positively influenced my state of mind, I came to a place of great fulfillment. Nowadays, my rituals bring me a sense of peace, grounding, love, and excitement. They have been essential to my spiritual awakening. The following are some examples of the rituals I use today to keep me connected to my spiritual truth. Look for ideas that speak to your own knowing. Your goal is not to engage in all the practices listed below. Instead, use the examples provided to help you uncover your own magical ritual recipe.

Water

When I wake up each morning, I drink a lot of water. This allows me to flush any toxins collected in my body overnight and begin the day well hydrated. Something I've learned about connecting with Spirit is that hydration is an absolute. For some reason, after a strong spirit connection, the body seeks to replenish itself. I've always been a water drinker, and now I see why.

Essential Oils

I began using essential oils long before they were trending because I've always been sensitive to smells. When I took classes to become certified as a massage therapist, our instructors advised us to work with specific types of oils. For example, they said we should never massage with mineral oil because our skin is our largest organ, and if we can't drink it, why would we want to absorb it into our skin? In reading Scripture, I also learned that oils have been used as a healing modality since antiquity.

For me, pure oils are so versatile because they are safe to ingest, inhale, and absorb. In the mid-nineties, I discovered a brand of pure oils that I love and trust and still use to this day. Oils have become an important ritual for me because they add flavor to my life. Their vibration is high, the smells are healing, and they make me happy. Here are some examples of how I use essential oils:

- I ingest lemon oil daily, adding it to my tea and water.
- I apply oils topically if there is an ailment to heal, or simply to enjoy a scent I love throughout the day. I love frankincense, ylang ylang, and lavender.

- I place oils in a diffuser to allow the smell to permeate throughout my home, and I breathe in the lovely scented oils.
- I ingest peppermint and rub lavender on every night before I go to bed.

Morning Prayer/Meditation

The act of morning meditation has become one of my most important rituals because every day it reminds me of who I am—my authentic self—and this life that I have chosen. There are so many ways to meditate. I'll share what I do each day, but please know that every form of meditation is good if it aligns with what feels right and best for you. Do you like music, guided imagery, binaural beats, or maybe total quiet? Or maybe a walk, hike or drive? Any or all of these things work when we are looking to get into a meditative state.

In the beginning, for me, a meditative state was best described as a mindset of relaxation. The more I meditated—typically using guided meditations from YouTube—the more I realized that I was drifting away from their guidance and settling into my own alternate dimensions. These days when I meditate, I fix some tea with lemon and then I gather my meditation stones and crystals and place them on either side of me. Once settled, I sit quietly, close my eyes, and just allow thoughts to come through and clear out. Then I ask myself, "What do I need to know today?" and I let my guidance take over. During meditation, I might say a mantra, pull an oracle card, move through my chakras, or do whatever I feel guided to do at the time. I have even texted a friend or two to let people know I'm thinking of them because it was what I felt guided to do.

Crystals and Stones

When I spent time at the ocean as a child, I always enjoyed collecting shells. They were a high vibration and a representation of life, and I loved them. So it's probably no surprise that I have a special connection with stones and crystals. I can feel the vibration in stones and crystals when I touch them. The stones and crystals I've collected over time represent the vibrational state I want to maintain. I've gathered these from around the world—Brazil, Croatia, Italy, and throughout the United States. Each stone and crystal is so different, and I honestly couldn't begin to describe the exact use of each one. Here are some examples of what I do with my stones and crystals:

- I keep them in special places around the house. I have them on each nightstand by the bed and strategically placed throughout different parts of my home in the kitchen, living room, and so on.
- I bring them in my purse and my car to have their vibration with me wherever I go.
- When I stay in a hotel or a friend's home, I sage the room to clear it of other energy, and I bring out my crystals and place them throughout the room.

Jewelry

I just love, love, love jewelry. Some of my crystals and stones live in my jewelry, but I have all kinds of other jewelry too. My jewelry defines my individuality. The ritual of getting dressed and deciding what jewelry to wear helps me express my individuality on that day, and it feels amazing. Don't be surprised to find me in big rings, large hoops and supersized gems whenever you meet me in person. I love it all.

The fun thing about jewelry is that not only is it decorative, it also serves as a spiritual connection. Some purposeful jewelry I have includes:

- Chakra rings – rings I can wear across my hands, each one representing a chakra.
- A necklace with embedded beads, with the prayer of St. Francis having been prayed over each bead as it was being crafted.
- Pieces of jade and lapis in the form of a necklace that carry vibrant colors and mystical energy.

Music

Where do I begin with music? I came out of the womb beating my own drum, and I have loved music every step along the way. I listen to it, I compose songs, I dance with it, and it makes me feel alive. I don't have a specific genre or type of music I like—I listen to it all. Ritually, I use music to lighten my vibration. I almost always have some type of music playing. Music can bridge gaps and make us feel connected to experiences; it helps us be present to what is happening at any given time. The intention of a song, no matter it's lyrics, exists to make a connection and support memory recall.

When I want to feel good, relax, sing, set the mood, dance, and even meditate—music is there for me.

Before Sleep Relaxation

For me, spiritual energy can make me feel giddy, like a kid in a candy store—wide awake and ready to jump and dance. This has been true my whole life, and so sleep has always been a bit of an afterthought. When I was around eight, my dad taught me a sleep relaxation technique that I have since modified and use nightly. Again, my practice may not be best for you, but the takeaway here is that a bedtime ritual can really help you settle into a good night's sleep so your body can be of service for a long and healthy life journey.

Before I get into bed, I place a drop of pure peppermint oil in my mouth and put lavender under my nose and near my ears. I put lotion on my feet, and I reach for my lip balm. I lay down and help my body get comfortable. To do this, I begin to think about my feet, and then I focus on each part of my body from toe to head until I feel really relaxed. I have some very old quotes that I love from some of my spiritual classes and books hanging above my bed, and I often read them to infuse my mind with those ideas as I drift off to sleep. If Spirit decides to begin communicating to me, I have learned to ask for the support the next day should sleep elude me.

Baths

For as long as I can remember, baths have been very important to me, a true sanctuary. I enjoyed long baths all throughout my marriage to my ex. My bath ritual was essential in keeping me spiritually on my path. As I began to explore different spiritual teachings, my baths became more than just relaxing; they became meditative. You might guess that, as a Spiritual Alchemist, my meditations are filled with all kinds of beautiful soul-beings and messages. And you'd be right!

The following are some examples of things that have happened in my baths.

In one bath, I lit a candle, and when I happened to open my eyes, the shower curtain made a silhouette of a face. In my childhood, I had always loved the bottle of maple syrup with the picture of Aunt Jemima, and I would stare at it for long periods of time. Interestingly, I remember being fascinated by syrup bottles in general after connecting with the Aunt Jemima bottle. Looking back, I realize I was probably exchanging non-verbal messages with what I have now come to understand as one of my first spirit guides. The syrup was my cue to tune in and listen to what was being shared. The energy came across as being a very kind, loving, and motherly energy.

That day in the bath, when the shower curtain silhouette looked just like Aunt Jemima—hair, headpiece, and all—I got very excited. I didn't quite acknowledge that she was a spirit guide; I simply felt joyful seeing the silhouette. After this Aunt Jemima bath, I kept hearing the song "Georgia" by Ray Charles whenever I listened to any kind of music. In my next bath, the silhouette came back, and I realized that she was talking with me. Soon enough, she told me that she was my spirit guide, and later she told me that her name was Georgia. Over time, she showed me unconditional love that I just kept feeling. Whenever her song played, or she came to me in or out of the bath, I felt very loved and at peace. She was a constant voice and always so loving, similar to what you might imagine a grandparent to be: your number one fan.

One day, she came to me and said good-bye, telling me her work was done and I had learned all that she wanted me to understand at that point. She validated for me that I was on my true, authentic path, and she encouraged me to continue forward on the path of self-love.

In another bath experience, I had just immersed as much of my face and body into the water as I could, when I felt a pressure on my chest that pushed me further down into the water. My face went under, and only my nose was outside of the water. I didn't panic, but my heart did skip a beat because I felt a presence that I did not recognize. I could see it, and it was enormous. It was a part of his knee that pushed me down into the water, and then I received a clear message about myself and direction. Because I was still trying to think while I was listening to the message, I didn't fully absorb it until later. When the being was done talking, I asked, "Who is this?" and he answered, "Azrael." I jumped out of the bath, ran to the computer and started searching for Israel because I hadn't heard the name Azrael before, and I assumed I had misunderstood. The search asked, "Did you mean Archangel Azrael?" When I clicked on yes, I was guided to an exact picture of the image that was shown to me in the bath. I cried. The picture validated that what I heard and saw was true.

Another archangel who came to visit me looked kind of like Jesus, but with red hair. I kept feeling pure love. I remember being in awe and asking repeatedly, "Who are you?" He said, "Archangel David." At the time, I had not heard of an Archangel named David. This time, my internet search resulted in nothing. So, I reached out to a person who channels archangels and asked him about David. He told me that he had not had an experience with an Archangel David, but that he would not be surprised to learn that new archangels would be revealed to people, given each individual's spiritual history. It is my experience that the David who came to me is the same David from the biblical Old Testament. And he was showing me a whole new aspect of pure love.

The funny thing about these rituals is that, when I'm in them, I am a totally vulnerable version of my human form. It is through these rituals that I receive validation messages of pure love. From the ritual practices, I have learned to love myself for who I am. If we don't understand ourselves enough to say "I love myself" in every circumstance, how can we ever imagine being able to give true love to another person? We must value it from within, for ourselves, in order to then bless others with our love.

Overcoming Judgment, Shame, and Guilt

When I was married, I hated tattoos. My husband had one tattoo in particular that I could barely tolerate, and when he wanted to make changes to it, I was adamant that the tattoo should get no time or attention. Years later, on our twenty-fourth wedding anniversary, we traveled to Mendocino, California, together. While there, we walked into a tattoo shop and I noticed my disdain was no longer present. I found myself appreciating the artistic aspects of the tattoos, and I felt a sense of understanding for the choice to tattoo oneself. At that point, I unexpectedly found myself supporting his desire to update his tattoo.

Later in the day, while my husband and I were walking on the property where we were staying for the night, I found a beautiful hawk feather. I grabbed it and brought it back to our quiet cottage, which consisted of one large open room with a kitchenette. Inside the cottage on the window sill of the largest window, there was a small bunch of sage into which I placed the feather. The feather and the sage were incredibly synchronous and would be of use in just a few hours.

The bed sat in the middle of the room, facing the large open window. We were messing around on the bed, and I felt like I was being watched. The cottage was on a second level, and the bed's headboard blocked the view to the door. I felt as though it could be a human watching, but there was no evidence that this was the case. And yet the sense of being watched was so strong, I had to ask my husband to stop. Then I started getting chills. The chills were so bad that my teeth were chattering and I could not speak, so my husband put the blankets on me to try and warm my body. This went on for about ten minutes.

When the shaking and chattering subsided, I got up and knew I had to sage the room. I grabbed the feather and the sage and quickly began smudging. This involved lighting the sage until it began to smoke and then using the feather to wave the sage smoke into the space. When I reached the glass door, on the opposite side of the room, I saw a demon. I said to it, "You look like something out of a movie I've seen." It had black horns coming out of its long, flat head. Its eyes were lit with red lights that looked like Christmas lights. I remember quietly talking to the demon out loud, saying, "I'm not afraid of you; you're not welcome here, the light resides here." I stood powerfully and stayed there, quietly speaking these and other words until he left. By the time I'd completed saging the room and got back into bed, my husband had already fallen asleep. He told me later that I had spent forty-five minutes on this task.

As I was lying in bed, I tried to reconcile what had happened. I still had no fear and was ready to drift off to sleep when the cottage shook. It felt like some kind of fight was going on outside. I saw that two entities who were clashing with each other had hit the house, causing the cottage to shake. I understood that this was a type of spiritual warfare. The demon had brought others. I felt my guides and angels winning the fight over the demons.

What I was experiencing was an outward manifestation of an inner battle. Because of my Christian background and a history of watching scary movies, I readily gave fear the face of a demon. In this outward battle, I was choosing to stop fear from ruling my life. I felt thankful to my angels and guides for this powerful demonstration.

After my second and final separation with my ex, it was shown to me in a meditation that the second man who raped me had arm tattoos. This helped me to see that my judgement of the tattoos was centered on my own shame. My shame resided in not acknowledging, or talking about, the sexual abuse of my early life. Over time, that shame bubbled up through my judgments around tattoos, porn, the sanctity of marriage, and so on.

Our judgment is so much more than a character or cultural preference; it lies deep within our knowing—a false truth of sorts. Today, the perspective I carry regarding the circumstances in that cottage is that it was not "a demon"—it was my ultimate fear demons. Outside, it was my collection of fears, represented as demons that I had carried up to that point, who were engaging in the spiritual warfare with my guides and angels. I no longer believe in evil. For me, evil is simply a form of fear. Thus, the demons were not evil; they were instead a reflection of my shame and guilt. In working to release all that no longer served me, I was doing the spiritual work. In that work, I had subconsciously invited my demons to present themselves and be cleared from my life. There is however negative energy which can rear its ugly head in the form of demons and otherworldly entities.

Consequently, to further my release, I have since gotten a tattoo. This thing I had judged with such vigor is now a part of me. Standing in my power in the cottage, getting my own tattoo, and even sharing this story with you, is all reflective of living in my truth without abandon.

In Part One, I described how I made the difficult decision to have an abortion at the age of eighteen. Since I was still in my numb, disassociated state, the choice was not difficult to make at the time. I didn't realize, though, how much guilt I carried around about having done it. I met my husband about four months after the procedure. He didn't understand how raw my emotions were, nor how guilty I felt. For years, I avoided dealing with how it made me feel or reconciling my decision.

When I got pregnant with my second child, all the home pregnancy tests were coming out negative. I went to the doctor and they ordered a blood test. This was more than four years after my abortion, and as synchronicity would have it, the office that I went to for the test was the same office that had been the abortion clinic. I hesitated even going in, but I needed to know for sure if I was pregnant. I went in with my five-month-old in tow. We didn't wait long, and when they escorted me to the exact same room that I'd had the procedure in, I got very pale, I could hardly talk, and my heart was pounding. I knew at that moment that I was pregnant and why. The technician asked me several times if I was okay and if I wanted to proceed. I just kept nodding yes. She took my blood, and I couldn't get out of there fast enough.

I had become a Christian the year before and I knew it was no mistake that I went there. I didn't address it for another couple of months, and then I started asking for clarification in my prayers. In my eighth month of pregnancy, I had a vision. I was sitting in a pew in a very big, beautiful church, crying, and a luminescent angel came down and sat in the pew slightly behind and to the side of me. This angel told me that I had not forgiven myself for the abortion, and that's why I was sent back to the clinic. I needed to face myself and let go. It was comforting to think that God had forgiven me, and so over the next month I practiced just that, letting it go. I knew I was being blessed with another child, and yet I instinctively knew that it was not the child from before.

This was further validated later when I met my never-born child and he told me his name was James. He came to me while I was getting my hair cut. Thank goodness I was at home and one of my sisters was doing my hair. My oldest daughter was there too. He told me that he had been with me the whole time and was very happy to finally talk to me. We talked for the next few days, and then agreed it was time for him to move on and go be with a wonderful family.

At a workshop I was hosting with a friend of mine, I received a profound realization. During a group meditation, as I was holding space and lifting my arms to the amazing energy all around me, a collective voice came to me and said, "Forgiveness is a farce." *What? What the hell? Are you kidding me? Wait—I am the queen of forgiveness. I've had to forgive so many people in my life to get here today.* I couldn't even talk to my guides. I just told them that I would have to get back to them. "Can't you see I'm right in the middle of something here?"

The workshop took a scheduled break, and I went to a room to try and get clarity about my beliefs around forgiveness. My guides began sharing with me that if we all have soul contracts, and those soul contracts have been achieved, what is there to forgive? We asked all those people to do, say, and be that way to help us learn life lessons. I knew I wouldn't change anything that had happened to me because it led me to where I am now. So, why did I feel the need to forgive them? I realized that if I wanted to forgive anyone, it would be myself. As you might expect, I'd developed anger instead of understanding because I was focused on forgiving others for their deeds. But then there are no mistakes, ever. So, why would I feel the obligation to forgive?

I realized at that moment that I should thank all those who seemingly hurt me for fulfilling exactly what we'd contracted. I started seeing how difficult asking these other souls to do this on my behalf must have been for them. The story of the Little Soul and the Sun by Neale Donald Walsch came to mind. The little soul wanted more than anything to experience forgiveness in its lifetime, but it needed another soul to offer themselves to be the offender. In the end, the Little Soul waited anxiously to be able to experience itself as forgiveness, and to thank whatever other soul made it possible. And at all the moments in that new lifetime, whenever a new soul appeared on the scene, whether that new soul brought joy or sadness (especially if it brought sadness), the Little Soul thought of what God had said. "Always remember, I have sent you nothing but angels."

Thanks to my guides, I was overwhelmed with this new understanding of forgiveness. I felt such gratitude that I now could look at everyone in such an unconditional, loving way. I encourage you to let go of shame, guilt and judgment. Every interaction is for our best and highest good. Whether someone caused you pain, or you caused them pain, it is now in the past. It was done to help your soul's evolution, and can be looked at with pure love. No matter what!

Maintaining Vibrational Frequency

Frequency maintenance is matching the vibration that comes out of each of us with the people we attract into our lives. We all have our own unique vibration. We share vibration with our children, spouse, pets, friends, coworkers, extended family, and so forth. When vibrational frequencies don't match anymore, that is when separation occurs. So often, people will work diligently to maintain the same vibration because we're afraid of the loss that might come from our organic change of frequency.

Our vibration affects everything. We are all energy, and energy carries a specific vibration. Sometimes we will see something that we are so attracted to that we must have it. This can be true for people as well as inanimate objects. That is an example of resonating with its vibration. Both are made up of pure energy.

If we try to keep ourselves at a lower vibration, so we can keep a relationship, at home or at work, it is a slow way of killing ourselves. The more we try to hide or cover our natural vibration, the more painful life feels. It's like trying to put lightning into a jar. We say we want joy, love, and happiness, and yet we try to obtain those things by keeping everything around us the same. If the lightning is stuffed in the jar long enough, the light begins to diminish.

I chose marriage because it seemed like a safe and logical step. After a rough set of early life circumstances, marriage felt stable. At the time, I was numb and disconnected from my emotional truth. I attracted a man that matched who I was during that period of my life. We then had three daughters and created a vibrational frequency for our family. We attracted friends and kept relationships with extended family who matched us all, and we maintained that frequency for twenty-five years. My lightning was in the jar, slowly dying all that time.

I never set out to change my family life. I was proud of my role in running a stable household. You can imagine, then, how conflicted I felt when it became clear that some of these relationships needed to change, or possibly end. The vibrational mismatch became more and more profound as I got my health on track, attended therapy, and sought out spiritual teachers. For a few years, I tried to hang on and make it all somehow fit together. I wanted to believe that I could grow spiritually and somehow "maintain" the status quo.

Interestingly, as we adjust our vibration, it influences those around us to raise theirs as well. An example is my relationship with my carpool buddy, JennMarie, who was instrumental in many of my early spiritual a-ha moments. We were raising our vibration together. A change doesn't always result in the end of a connection. Sometimes, it can strengthen a relationship, as it did for JennMarie and me during that time.

In the case of my marriage, an ending was inevitable. My spouse was as clear about keeping his frequency as I was clear in evolving mine. Adjusting our vibration can seem like a selfish thing to do. It requires us to be honest with what is necessary to honor and love ourselves. This seems to contradict everything I had been taught about my responsibilities as a woman, wife, and mother. Yet, when we start honoring our vibrational truth, it is the most freeing, fun, and loving thing we can do. There is difference between self-care and selfishness. Narcissism is defined as an unhealthy obsession with oneself; this is not what I'm suggesting. Honoring our truth simply requires us to be tuned into and attentive to our unique vibrational frequency.

When we consider the vibrational chart, we have to wonder who doesn't want to live in bliss. I know I do. I set my intentions on living a blissful life. In addition to the dissolution of my marriage, my relationships with friends and extended family have evolved too, and I have come to learn they are always evolving. Even in times of stagnancy, our vibrational frequency is constantly choosing its closest match. Go ahead and take an inventory of the frequency matches surrounding you now. What is the vibrational frequency in your immediate family, your work, your friends, your neighbors, your extended family? What are they showing you about yourself?

During the early stages of my awakening, I actively sought a mentor, thinking I needed someone to show me how to be my spiritually awakened self. It sounds funny when I write this now because only I can be myself, right? And, as the frequency law would have it, the more I tried to "find" people in my frequency, the more lost I felt.

If you take a group of kids and add one child who is older or younger than the group, that child will take on the vibration of the group. For example, if the child joining the group is younger, he or she will start acting older. If the group is younger, an older child will start acting younger. We are absolutely influenced by one another, and we have a responsibility to become fully aware of the vibrational frequency we choose all the time.

Vibrational frequency is contagious, and each of us has an opportunity to positively influence our life based on the frequency we tune into. As they say, the shortest distance between two people is a smile. We can change somebody's day simply by managing our own vibrational frequency. It is not someone else's fault when you are going through something. Handing off a negative vibrational frequency only opens the door for more negativity. Let's stop tuning into the frequency of pain and upset. Instead, let's choose to share joy and bliss.

Releasing Addiction to Comfort

One of the biggest challenges we face is our innate desire to be comfortable. We strive for comfort every day. Parking spots, cubicles, dinner choices, and seminar seats—we prefer to be comfortable. Living an authentic life is risky.

If you wake up every morning and genuinely feel that you love the life you are living, and you feel authentic all the time, that's awesome—you can skip to the conclusion of this book. But if you wake up and feel there is something more awaiting you, then consider the dangers of complacency.

I am committed to our collective spiritual growth. We're committed to everyone else—family, work, community—and we do everything we can for them, and then we give up on ourselves. Look at New Year's resolutions, for example. Each year we promise ourselves a healthier version of ourselves, and then give up on the idea within days or weeks.

Even when we carry a nagging feeling inside of us, a desire for something more, humans just naturally fail to act. We fill our lives with all kinds of tasks, telling ourselves that busy work must get done for us to survive. Maybe it's about paying rent, or getting the kids into the right school, or finding a new business connection.

Many clients come to me with questions about their lives, wondering what might happen in a certain situation. While it might be helpful to get situational clarity at times, this can distract us from recognizing when we have become too comfortable with the status quo of our lives. By focusing on the drama of the moment, our ego convinces us to stay in place and keep repeating the same patterns over and over again. Complacency is an overused form of self-protection.

Yes, sometimes our fears hold us back, and we let fear choose the same comfortable path. It's more than that, though. Being comfortable is possibly more dangerous than fear. Not the physical "run for your life" kind of danger, dangerous in the sense that it will deprive us from truly living. Being comfortable nearly killed me. I lived in a house so full of mold that I could barely breathe for almost a year. Yet, of all the things I did to fix the breathing problem, making a big life change was not something I was ready to consider. I had worked so hard to create a stable life, to have my children feel loved; changing that seemed to go against everything I had worked so hard to achieve. As it turns out, the opposite was true. The thing I needed most was change—to become a more authentic version of myself. Instead, I stayed in the religion, and I stayed in the marriage.

For complete candor, I had always known that it was not likely we would stay married. It was a feeling I'd secretly held from early in the relationship. I used the doctrine of religion to help me avoid this feeling, and told myself that the feeling was not okay and needed to be pushed away. I looked outside of myself to everyone else's expectations to help me decide how to live.

I laugh at myself now when I think about how I initially approached my spiritual awakening. I was once again looking outside of myself. I remember trying desperately to get the guidelines of spirituality the way I'd found guidelines in Christianity. I was a good Christian, so my goal was to be a good at being spiritually awake. I pursued courses and certifications everywhere I could—Deborah King life energy courses, Collette Baron-Reid's oracle card reading, Hay House teachers, Spiritual Life Coaching certification including Quantum Process, Neuro Linguistic Programming, and Meditation. I did lots and lots of reading. It was all helpful in opening my channels of thought, but it was clear that there is not only one way to be spiritually awake. In the end, some of what I read was a great fit to my authentic self, and some of it just didn't apply to me.

Initially, I tried to make all of what I was learning work for me. I would try the daily rituals, prayers, or meditations that my co-learners raved about. All along, I kept telling myself that I was committed to finding my truth. This commitment carried me forward into more and more experiences that were out of this world—from meditative memories and visions to archangel visits and more. Not everyone will have a memory recall moment that shakes up their whole life like I did, but I do believe that we must be committed to our own individual truths. The awakening is ongoing and unique for each one of us.

My Sexual Awakening

When I separated from my husband, I had no intentions of looking for someone in my life. In fact, I focused solely on my emotional well-being. It was and is all about my soul's growth. Well, what I didn't realize was that part of MY healing/growing was truly, in the words of Marvin Gaye, "Sexual Healing."

Up to this point, even with all I had experienced sexually, I didn't realize how positive and desirable sex truly felt. During the times of promiscuity in my youth, I was numb to the emotions and feelings of sex acts. Once I married, it was my wifely duty for the length of the marriage. It's not that I didn't enjoy it, just not all of the time. Toward the end, I was drinking wine more frequently just to be able to have sex with him. Open, honest sex was not available to me until after our separation. When I chose to want to know myself and love myself, that in turn required me to understand the sexual side of myself.

Many of us have been given directives from parents, religion, school, and society at large regarding sex. Here are some of the messages I heard growing up:

- We give ourselves away when we just have sex with someone.
- Sex shouldn't be done out of wedlock.
- Only "sluts" sleep with someone they don't really know.

Stepping outside of these beliefs and awakening to my sexual self has been exhilarating, fun, and deeply emotional. It did not require me to sleep with an army of strangers, but I did have to step out of my comfort zone in many ways.

HOW DID YOU DO THIS, WITH WHOM, HOW DID YOU KNOW YOU COULD TRUST HIM?

I was driven by fear when it came to all aspects of sex. Fear that it could be enjoyable, when I had never experienced it in that way. It was a simple yes to allow myself to go have some fun with someone.

When I traveled to India in late 2017, many wonderful things happened, and one very significant one changed me from the inside out. Part of the trip involved staying at a temple and partaking in a tantric workshop. The whole experience was surreal, especially experiencing the Kalavahana Puja, an empowerment ritual. Someone from the workshop was there to assist and work the energy for working on the chakras.

We changed our clothes into what resembled mumus for the women and cloth for the men. Each ritual required four participants, and my ritual had three women and one man. As soon as the women helpers started chanting and my helper started touching my body, I went into a sacred space. The chants sounded farther away, and I was aware of my body, but not really in my body. My breathing became erratic and the tears started flowing. I had no relation as to why this was happening, and I couldn't stop crying. What seemed like a really long time ended up only being about twenty minutes. The women helpers asked if I was okay, which I was except for the stream of tears that had not stopped. I quickly got dressed, grabbed my shoes, and away I went.

I felt as though I were floating. I couldn't feel the ground, rocks, or anything else under my feet. I didn't know where I was going either. Something drew me to another building, and as I was walking up to it, I stopped about halfway and asked if the crying was ever going to stop. One of the cooks was walking past and asked if I was all right, to which I replied I was fine. He told me I was not fine and held out a key.

Each smaller worship temple was behind a locked gate. I knew he was handing me the key to go into the temple farther up the hill. As I trekked up, out of breath from my tears and erratic breathing, I unlocked the door to a very holy place. I wasn't sure what I was doing, and I could smell and see the cook's offering at the base of the

Goddess room. My spirit guides then guided me to go around the to the side of the room. As I reached the outside of the small room's wall toward the back of the temple, there was a very large, Shiva Lingham (see pictures below) almost as big as I am (which is 5'4" on a good day).

I was facing the sculpture when I heard the words, "Sit on it." WHAT? Again, "Sit on it." After hearing the words a third time, I obeyed, first making sure no one else was entering the temple.

Now to sit on it actually meant that I would be straddling the bottom part. Then I heard, "Hug it." WHAT? In my mind, I was thinking, *They want me to hug a big dick. I came all the way to India to hug a big dick.* And yet, I knew that there was more to this than that, and so I reached my arms around the sculpture. As I hugged it, I felt an intense heat coming up through my legs. In India, the female area is called *yoni* (which is what I now call it myself), and that heat was coming right up through my yoni. Next I started to see a kind of newsreel with pictures of the first time I was molested at age two and continuing through my whole life. Each reel represented a negative sexual experience in my life. As each reel popped up, I literally saw a finger pushing a delete button.

As soon as the reel finished and the last delete was hit, my crying stopped. The faucet stopped and this light started coming out of me, starting in my lower parts. I knew it was my kundalini even though I didn't know much about it. I could feel my kundalini opening and the light emanating from it. A beautiful mantra started playing in my head: "Your yoni remembers, your yoni remembers . . ." I felt an immense love for the sensual, sexual side of me that I had not yet known.

After starting to play around with sex and feeling all the new things I had not allowed myself to experience, I started having fun. Even using my vibrator was different and more exciting. I was very honest with myself and sometimes fell back into my old routine. It was a learning process and one that I was willing to dive deeper into. Having my yoni remember helped me realize how much I was still "doing" and not receiving. Learning to receive affected everything—how I talked, sexting, wearing sexy bras and panties, and realizing how much I love kissing. It was all so good because I had never experienced this before.

As I became more aware of what I wanted in a partner, I had to start thanking the experiences I had and then let go of them. They had been so much fun and I had learned so much and I was so thankful I had someone to share it with, and yet I learned to be okay with letting the person go. It was very freeing. Our minds can play the emotions card and we can feel sucked in again, but in all reality, it's just an attachment—an attachment to feeling that someone loves or cares for you, or even someone to just hug and kiss you. When I released the attachment, so went all the emotional baggage with it.

Are we meant to be with someone forever? Is marriage the only way to say, "This is how much I love you?" Does a ring signify that I am bound to some type of law that prevents me from realizing that I am attracted to another?

These are all personal questions, and at the same time, questions we as a society need to discuss more. I now understand that what attracts us to each other is all energy. We connect energetically as does the whole universe. Allowing ourselves to grow and expand with each other is the gift of love we give one another. I feel there is so much negativity surrounding our sexuality, especially women. Men are exemplified as the more sexual beings, yet when I was coming into my sexually knowing, I wanted it all the time and did so for thirty-one nights in a row (something I didn't know my body was capable of, let alone want it that much).

I knew that when I opened myself up to receiving sexual healing, I would need to keep reminding myself to be honest about the fact that this was all about me—honoring, loving, and getting to know myself.

Conclusion

Many say that our knowing is instinct, intuition, or even a gut feeling. It's a feeling inside of us that tells us something is inherently true, even when outward circumstances suggest differently. What I have learned is that it's this innate truth within us that serves as the ultimate guide. We know what we know, and we can't un-know it. If we all stood together in our knowing, we would all come together in understanding that this life is about love.

In my role as a Spiritual Alchemist, I often give one-on-one or group readings. At the start of the reading, I always say, "I am only here to confirm what you already know." I started saying this early on in my career because it is important for me to confirm for people that they already have their truth inside of them. My clients, like all of us, are always being guided to find their truth, their voice, their bliss, and ultimately live a life of love.

Too often we take our knowing for granted. We disregard it as unhelpful, or as some type of annoying burden. We all know which way to go or how to handle situations or people, but we allow other factors to invade that knowing. We dismiss our inner truth, tell ourselves we are crazy, weird, or that it was luck or a fluke. When we read newspapers, magazines, books, or watch TV, we let other people tell us what to think or feel. We strive to follow what the media or our culture tells us we should do or have. When we get all of our messages from external sources, we are abandoning ourselves.

Throughout all the years of my marriage, I had a knowing that I would not be married for the rest of my life. I knew that we wouldn't retire together. I even knew that the time of separation would be after my children were capable of moving out on their own. Does that make the marriage wrong or bad? No, it was our journey to be married for that long. I had the knowing from the start, yet I didn't acknowledge it or make it my truth until I began the work of self-care, and learned to live a more authentic life.

Our role in understanding our knowing is to see love more expansively. All actions must be centered in love. When we shop for clothes, it is because we love the idea of finding a favorite piece of clothing that feels good on our skin. When we pick up groceries, we enjoy the experience of finding foods that delight our senses and nourish our body. When we take a call from a treasured friend, it is because we love hearing news of their wonderful life. When we watch a favorite TV show, it is because we love the characters and get excited about how it will all play out. If you are shopping, talking, and watching TV without that overwhelming feeling of love, you are out of alignment with your knowing. Doing things out of old habits that have long since lost their joy is breaking all us apart.

We evolve around love. As we grow through experiences, how we love must be free of labels, rules, and judgments. We must be free to evolve in love. Something we may have disliked early in life can become a favorite thing later in life, if we allow it to become so. Too often, we disregard our changing preferences and desires because we are afraid to rock the boat or disrupt what has become our status quo. Instead of living a life of love we become, in the words of Pink Floyd, "comfortably numb."

There are things we know about ourselves. I have always been good with numbers, for example. Being good with numbers could have led me to an accounting career, but that never felt quite right. I have always been super encouraging. I always enjoyed interacting with fellow humans. Customer service came so easy to me that I never had to think about doing it; it was just who I was. I know I'm a good listener. Many of these traits might even put me in a category as an empath, which I don't disagree with. Yet, my knowing suggested that my life's work would be made up of more than just these characteristics. Think of characteristics and skills as labels, helpful tools to show you what you love, but not an identity on which to get stuck. Too often, we find a label we like and stay stuck there long after we no longer love it.

Facebook really put this in perspective for me when they released the love emoji. I had more than 1,200 "loves," compared with a dozen or so "likes." I love everything. Someone eats a good meal, goes to a show, logs in and says hi—whatever they're doing, I love it! We have been given this lifetime because we have chosen to experience love. Gratitude is love. Quoting Bob Marley, "Love the life you live; live the life you love." That is living from our place of knowing.

When I was going from teacher to teacher to teacher during the early stages of my spiritual quest, it was because I was constantly seeking to confirm what aligned with my knowing. So many things I was taught felt true, while others not so much. Eventually, I stopped seeking their experiences to teach me what to think or feel, and I started relying on my own knowing. The more I trusted myself, the more open my spiritual connection became and the more magical my life became.

I am not any different from you. At some point, we must all take time to quiet the external noise and look inside of ourselves for the truth that is ours alone. My truth and experiences will never be yours, and yours will never be mine. Thus, learning to trust the knowing within, to pursue love over all else, is essential for living an awakened life.

PART THREE: My Invincible Love

Introduction

For many years, I have had an understanding that I would write three books. It was clear that at least one of the books would involve my chaotic life history. Beyond that, the specifics of the works were not revealed to me until I began writing. One of the most important concepts brought forth is that time is not linear. This has evolved into a collective of three small books in one volume representing the past, present, and future. 'My Invincible Truth' shared stories of my chaotic early life. It was my personal history, one that once held shame and judgment and is now one of love and gratitude. 'My Invincible Awakening' shared examples of how I came to live a blissful life through spiritual awakening. It reflects the daily practices I engage in to stay fully awake in every aspect of this human experience. This third part is 'My Invincible Love', a guidebook for the future. It shows us what we need to know to love ourselves and others while living life to its fullest expression.

In walking an awakened path, my soul is constantly evolving. The more I stand in my truth, the more I find myself opening to new beliefs and experiences. Each opening also brings a shift in my life circumstances and relationships. I have learned that I will not know all the details, yet I am certain it will all work out. I have found myself wondering how to stay in love with the naysayers; how to stay in truth in every action and reaction (mine and others); how to navigate the uncertainty.

I have come to learn that the path forward is paved with infinite possibilities. There are no missteps; every step leads us forward. Our soul's evolution is the only constant. You may remember from Book Two that I love music. I often write songs; fun or sentimental lyrics flow effortlessly out of me, and I write them joyfully in my journal. One song I wrote is called "Mama's Boy." It's an especially funny song about a mama who never approves of her son's romantic interests. His girlfriends are not good enough for her boy. To foster collaboration while writing this book, my dear friend and I took a road trip together. We were finishing Book One: My Invincible Truth, and we took a break to talk about music. I shared the lyrics to "Mama's Boy," and together we were overwhelmed with the a-ha moment that had James, my unborn child, been born, he could have been my mama's boy. Would I still be me? Yes, and no. My soul would still have its evolutionary growth. Yet the outer circumstances could have looked significantly different.

Knowing that every step we take is a right step is remarkably freeing. It can also be a bit overwhelming. In a society where we are constantly seeking the guidelines and evidence for what we need to do, say, or be to live a righteous life, it is easy to lose ourselves. I tried to be a good Christian/wife/mother, and then I tried to be a good seeker, and none of those could satisfy every question in my heart. In the end, I realized the only person who knows the truth for me, for my soul, is *me*—just as the only person who knows the truth for your soul *is* you.

There are not enough words to describe the magic that has occurred to bring these works to fruition. While "My Invincible Truth" and "My Invincible Awakening" were both written with Spirit's guidance, many of the words and examples were mine under divine guidance. The sections below are different. "My Invincible Love" has been predominantly channeled by Spirit. I have done my best to make a distinction between my words and the words of the spiritual teachers who chose to contribute. This entire book is a set of divine revelations.

Pure Love

I've said it before, and now is an opportunity to say it again. I have been guided to tell you that there is nothing in this book that you need to know. The only thing to know is that you are love. Your willingness to love yourself—to love every decision, every action, every inaction, every experience and every part of your life—is the only thing you need to know. Just love.

So, then you may be wondering why I am sharing this. Because you can make this bliss up! For me, I am giving you everything I have learned. It is within my knowing to extend this energetic vibration to touch your heart and expand our collective love.

We're often told not to be selfish. It's something we're taught as kids, and a message that gets stated repeatedly. "Don't be selfish," we're told. Yet selfishness is only a problem if it excludes the well-being of others. Pure love, on the other hand, is loving and nurturing oneself, while still maintaining a compassionate heart.

Let me give you some examples of what pure love looks like.

In "My Invincible Awakening," I shared information about my love of self-care rituals like meditation, nature walks, tea, essentials oil, etc. Specifically, the ritual of bathing has become one of the most important things I do because it exhibits pure love for myself in a way that harms no others and brings me great guidance and tranquility. As result, after my bath I am more attentive, clear-minded, and peaceful when interacting with others.

Another personal example of pure love is my vocal expression through music. I love to write songs, sing, and dance. I can be home alone or in a group of people, and when I hear a favorite song, I jump up and shake my head, dance, and sing. Sometimes it makes my friends laugh just hearing and seeing the fun I'm having. This makes my heart happy, which in turn raises my vibration. I feel great and then continue to spread pure love. Pure love is without restrictions, attachments, or cords of expectation.

At one point, I made a significant life decision to end my marriage. This, too, was an example of pure love. As I look back now, I see that there were opportunities for me to leave sooner, but I didn't love myself enough to go. I was able to walk away from the dysfunction only when I came to a point in my life when I finally believed that who I was mattered.

While writing this book, three Apostles spoke to me, explaining that they had worked together collaboratively when they wrote their own biblical verses. Peter, Paul, and John stated that they wanted to contribute toward what was being shared in this book. While writing this section on love, the following came through from the Apostle John.

The Apostle John

People want to use Yeshua as an example of pure love. And Yeshua would say, "God is love." Yeshua, yes, would identify himself as love and yet, if we look at his life, there were only three and a half years from the start to the end of his ministry. By the time he became enlightened, he had already become love. He had unconditional love for the people because he had unconditional love for himself.

Prior to his ministry, Yeshua was a man who worked as a carpenter, and who had life experiences as we all do. Yeshua had love of his family, respect for his parents, and yet, knew he was different and didn't fit the norm. So how then do we define love? If we asked people, what would they offer as the first word to describe love? We all have a different word. To fully love is to not give ourselves away. We share our love.

I wanted to channel this with you [Andrea] as I know you speak with Yeshua. I come with the energy knowing this truth, the truth of pure light. I saw a man who had accomplished the overcoming of life circumstances, to transcend norms and expectations to do what he was put on earth to do. There are many amazing examples of masters who have ascended past the circumference of human existence. While they were here, they were able to accept and receive themselves, and sought to raise their vibration, lift themselves up, and to be that love.

Some examples of ascended masters may include Buddha, Quan Yin, Mother Theresa, Jesus, Yogananda, Meher Baba, and so forth.

I know they call my book the love gospel, and I recognize that I was a very loving man, and I loved women. I actually resonated with Solomon's books when I read them because he too learned to love fully. When God asked Solomon what he wanted, God told him you can have anything and asked what will it be? Solomon said he wanted to be wise. In all reality being wise is having an understanding, and when you have an understanding how the universe works, then you understand it is about love. And, that is when Solomon really opened up and loved the people and they loved him.

You, Andrea, use your abilities to share messages that are for the love of the people. As a messenger, you make that your one constant. It's not about change. If we could stop focusing on trying to change things about ourselves, and instead just start loving ourselves, everything else comes exactly as it is supposed to. There is nothing for us to do or to make happen. If we start loving ourselves, there are so many possibilities that come forth. We can imagine it but we choose not to. Everybody is an ascended master, an apostle, a divinely anointed soul with a difference to make. This is where positive affirmations are vital.

Love is not formattable. Society wants everything to be a "how-to" guide in a 30-second ad; the quick fix. If we keep focusing on trying to create process steps or a how-to for everything we want to create or do, then we end up actually losing source. This, in turn, leaves us dissatisfied. We lose our connection to satisfaction. This is why so many people feel dissatisfied with their life partners, their work, their families and their life circumstances. We are losing our sense of what really makes us feel whole.

We are a throwaway society. Including throwing ourselves out. We're constantly trying to throw away the parts of ourselves that we don't like or don't approve of. This is judgement. We must stop trying to change or fix ourselves, we must learn to love all parts of ourselves.

Marriage is an institution. It is not necessarily love. It has been treated more as a business, and we have set up society to believe that it is necessary. Andrea was told she could not buy a car until she was married, she made a business decision. The love that we find in others, that we so love, is a reflection of ourselves. So, when we feel our business partner seeks love elsewhere [the cheater], we experience it as a loss of identity. Sex is not a sacred act. It is a physical act that can have an immense energetic exchange, and because that feels good we want to call it love. If there is no love for self, then the basket is empty. When we have love of self, everything is pleasurable and everything is excitable. As a society we sell the ideas of pleasure and excitement because that supports the business mentality. In buying the end product, we lose the ingredient that is most essential; love of self. – John

When the Apostle John shared this message, I remembered studying the Bible during my marriage. During the studies, I frequently wondered aloud why the Bible was filled with quotes from Jesus like, "If I can do this, you can do this," but no one was doing it. When I posed this question, people would respond by saying, "Well, we're all going to sin." I think they may have assumed I was speaking about being more compassionate or caring for one another. But actually, I was wondering about all things. Why can't we heal ourselves or one another? Why don't we perform miracles? So, when Apostle John came through on this day, it reminded me that we really can do everything he said we can do, including love with all of our being.

Shortly after this channeling with the Apostle John, I was visited by another divine guide. This was an Egyptian Goddess, Seshemi. I immediately got on the internet to try and find out who she was before I even heard her message. I felt that she was Egyptian, but I had some difficulty with her pronunciation since it was new to me. After a few short minutes, she shared the following message:

Seshemi, Daughter of Setankhu – Thirteenth Dynasty

In Egypt at that time, it was even more of a business. It was a transaction for the benefit of procreation. You would look for someone who would pass down good genetics. If you found someone that you loved in life, you almost never saw those two people together in marriage, nor in extramarital relations. If it did happen that two people pursued love, then it was a long fight for them to be together.

[Andrea's comment – I believe the long fight was due to societal expectations, traditions of the time.]

You see that kind of love, you go to all ends of the earth to have with another human being, exchanging a very sensitive and secret vibration that only these two people know. We had pleasurable moments (she showed a visual of an orgy; a group of men and women pursuing sexual/sensual pleasures together) because we were able to separate the business of the marriage from the pleasures of the body. We were raised knowing that we were all unique and powerful people.

Therefore, we loved ourselves and always took care of ourselves and thought of ourselves first. Yes, it was taken to the extreme by some and wars broke out, then division happened. The word that you describe as selfish, or the other word narcissism, can be taken to the extreme in the flick of a moment.

You today, have more women in power than any other civilization, and at the same time have more women who are lost and unloving of themselves. When you know the two are one, power and self-care, then amazing thrusts of loving emotion will occur. These emotions need to be expressed lovingly.

[In Egyptian times], you know the reason that a lot of things were buried with families is because we wanted to have the things around us that we loved. Like a special cup, a bowl or a staff. The family member chose the item because it had emotional power in it because it was so loved. If you drank from the cup that gave you youth, you loved it and it loved you. Thus, who would want to be without these items? – Seshemi

In "My Invincible Awakening" I shared a story about knowing that my marriage was never meant to be forever. I always knew, but I didn't want to admit it to myself or anyone. So, it was revealing when both the Apostle John and Seshemi referred to marriage as a business decision, because in hindsight, that was exactly how it felt. Before my divorce, I went to the Christian religion for sanctuary, and I found teachings that kept me imprisoned in something that I just knew wasn't right. According to my religious teachers, Malachi 2:16 points out that God hates divorce, and that was further evidence for me to stay bound to a commitment my younger self made. Now, through my spiritually awakened lens, I see the actual verse in an entirely new way. And this doesn't just apply to this Scripture verse; I find it to be true in so many more Scripture passages as well.

"The man who hates and divorces his wife," says the LORD, the God of Israel, "does violence to the one he should protect." (Malachi 2:16, NIV)

It goes back to what Seshemi said. We attribute loving feelings with another person in an effort to make ourselves feel whole. What actually happens in marriages that begin with a lack of self-love is that we divorce ourselves when we enter into that marriage. We lose sight of who we are and therefore are unloving with ourselves, each other, and the business transaction of the marriage. Think of it: jobs, mortgage, retirement savings, families, other assets and liabilities—marriage really *is* a business, isn't it? Love, on the other hand, is so much more.

The idea that God wanted me to stay miserable never made sense. And when I tried to seek evidence that a doomed marriage was what he wanted for me, I still felt confused. Today, I understand the Malachi verse to mean that hatred is of great concern for all of us, no matter what happens. If there is hate and violence from either party, in any relationship, we are experiencing the opposite of love. Hatred and violence stem from not loving ourselves. Staying in an oppressive relationship is not loving oneself. Divorce itself is not the problem; hatred and violence is of utmost concern to our spiritual selves. The more spiritually awakened I became, the more my heart sought love in every situation. My marriage was fraught with emotional and mental abuse, and I had become attached to playing the role of the victim. We spent over twenty years playing out these roles for one another, until I was finally able to listen to the knowing I'd always had.

When I met my ex-husband, I was very fit and worked out regularly. I have always been on the go, and evening workouts were a part of my instinctive need to stay busy. In that first year of marriage, until my pregnancy, I worked out consistently. After my first child was born, I got pregnant again, and then again. I waited ten years to attempt to reinstate my gym routine. Not surprisingly, that attempt was short-lived because I was using weight as an armor of self-protection, as a way of holding on to something that needed to be released long ago. When my ex and I separated, the release of the painful commitment led to a significant loss of weight. I went down dress sizes, from a size 22 to a size 14.

You might think my body issues went away completely with that immediate and unplanned weight loss. However, that was just the beginning of the lessons that would come through the awakening process. I find that this premise of pure love is one that requires constant nurturing. If I lose sight of the love even for a minute, it is easy to fall back into old patterns. The good news is that we can quickly catch the signs if we fall off track. If there is violence, hatred, or suffering, we are not in a state of love. If there is gratitude, appreciation, and compassion, then we are experiencing pure love. Pure love is nothing you must earn, nor is it a destination to reach. Pure love is who you are right now.

Truth

There is truth, and then there is truth—just as we say there are white lies, and then there is lying. We all have an inherent understanding of our Soul's truth that we sometimes choose to deny. Some people may pride themselves in being honest, but are we really being honest if we are not living in our truth? This chapter is about revealing our identity, our authentic self. It's about going deeper than just the surface behaviors of honesty or integrity. It is about living in our truth 100 percent of the time.

As a seeker myself, I spent twenty-two years of my life seeking truth in Scripture. I sought truth in churches, fellow worshippers, Christianity, and anything that I thought would bring me closer to the revelation of truth. Earlier when I spoke about becoming a Christian, which involves saying the Lord's Prayer for salvation, I told the ladies there that I didn't care who was on the pulpit or teaching, I just wanted to know the truth. I didn't know my own truth, so I was looking for truth in others, in other religions, and other ideas. In reality, the truth was, and is, in me. And ultimately that is what I have come to understand many ascended masters, angels, and guides are clearly saying to each of us.

When I set out to write a chapter on truth, I imagined I'd be talking about having truthful conversations, speaking my truth, and honoring my truth. However, those ideas were already captured in Book One, "My Invincible Truth." I should have expected that there was an opening here for a whole new level of understanding with regard to truth and love. This new level of understanding came through the Apostle Paul, followed by the Apostle Peter, who joined me while writing this chapter.

The Apostle Paul

Living our Truth

I was always a dignified man in Scripture, as they say. I had knowledge and understanding of what the surface life was supposed to be and look like. I had heard the stories that were being told of this man, Yeshua, and just couldn't believe that they were actually true. I actually crossed paths with Yeshua several times, that I did not put into my books. I wanted to observe the man. I sought him out, and I had to change my identity in order to get somewhat close to him.

[He showed me a visual of a courtyard, where he was not in close proximity or in the same room, but standing in the courtyard watching from a distance.]

I never saw him doing anything out of the ordinary, or perform any miracles, so my mind turned him into a cult leader. Someone taking people from a life that could be good for them. Do not think I didn't study what was written in the Scriptures about him previously. But as we all do, from my time to today, we see what we want to see, and read what we want to read. I justified some of the teachings and writings to fit my agenda. And, yet, my heart always knew a truth—that the man didn't have anything and wasn't asking for anything, so why would so many people follow him?

[He literally showed me people following Jesus from city to city; sitting with him, and sometimes words were never spoken.]

I am giving this account because I was an outsider. Some of my writings of these observations can be found under a different name in scrolls that are yet to be unearthed. You would call it a journal today because it was not a letter to anyone in any city. They were my own personal observations that I wrote down.

At this time there were so many other teachers. We had always known of these other Gods, priestesses and such. We knew the writings from our Ancients; these things were passed down.

[He showed me older writings, like hieroglyphics and texts which suggested that an enlightened being would come.]

To have a man with nothing, claim to have enlightenment and understanding into people; we were all very suspicious. There were many enlightened beings on the planet, they were just not in proximity, at a distance, far away. We were going through great trials and tribulations as individual segmented areas.

[It felt like he was showing me what looked like countries, but not the ones we know now. Some were bigger and different.]

A man with no horse is a man with no heart, meaning that if we did not have the freedom to go and travel and experience each other in an enlightened way, we lost our souls and our truth of who we were. And this one, Yeshua, brought it back to where we were. You know of these other ancient texts; the writings of enlightenment have been there all along. You know of the denial that is not only happening in your day, but in centuries past. There are always men looking to be the ruler over other men, so in the fight to the top, one loses self.

When I Met Yeshua on That Road

[Andrea comment: Biblical Scripture, Acts 9:3-20, tells the story of the road Damascus.]

I became a separated man. I knew it to be true and my surface-self denied it. I immediately felt that my denial, what you call ego, was the dark side of me, and my soul longed for the light. When my sight was released from me, it was because I could go inside and search myself.

The man that I met, to help me regain my sight, taught me many things, and made much sense. He should have been a greater public speaker, and yet he knew that his true self was to lay and wait for me, so after that moment he, in turn, would be even a greater light. You [Andrea] say miracles and magic are happening every day. It's moment by moment. It did not take me long to understand what that enlightenment meant for me. All the ancient texts that I had read to bring me great knowledge with the enlightenment made sense, and so they become one with me.

Acts 9:3-20 New International Version (NIV)

[3] As he neared Damascus on his journey, suddenly a light from heaven flashed around him. [4] He fell to the ground and heard a voice say to him, "Saul, Saul, why do you persecute me?"

[5] "Who are you, Lord?" Saul asked.

"I am Jesus, whom you are persecuting," he replied. [6] "Now get up and go into the city, and you will be told what you must do."

[7] The men traveling with Saul stood there speechless; they heard the sound but did not see anyone. [8] Saul got up from the ground, but when he opened his eyes he could see nothing. So they led him by the hand into Damascus. [9] For three days he was blind, and did not eat or drink anything.

[10] In Damascus there was a disciple named Ananias. The Lord called to him in a vision, "Ananias!"

"Yes, Lord," he answered.

[11] The Lord told him, "Go to the house of Judas on Straight Street and ask for a man from Tarsus named Saul, for he is praying. [12] In a vision he has seen a man named Ananias come and place his hands on him to restore his sight."

[13] "Lord," Ananias answered, "I have heard many reports about this man and all the harm he has done to your holy people in Jerusalem. [14] And he has come here with authority from the chief priests to arrest all who call on your name."

[15] But the Lord said to Ananias, "Go! This man is my chosen instrument to proclaim my name to the Gentiles and their kings and to the people of Israel. [16] I will show him how much he must suffer for my name."

[17] Then Ananias went to the house and entered it. Placing his hands on Saul, he said, "Brother Saul, the Lord—Jesus, who appeared to you on the road as you were coming here—has sent me so that you may see again and be filled with the Holy Spirit." [18] Immediately, something like scales fell from Saul's eyes, and he could see again. He got up and was baptized, [19] and after taking some food, he regained his strength.

Saul spent several days with the disciples in Damascus. [20] At once he began to preach in the synagogues that Jesus is the Son of God.

It is not to follow a man; it is to follow a truth. And following that truth, we stand up for it, because it is a truth within us. And, you [Andrea] have said numerous times from the beginning in two different ways: "I just want to know the truth," and, "It needs to make sense to me." Because truth is sense. Take your pieces sporadically off a puzzle and lay them on a table, and tell me what the picture is. Without having some type of guidebook, and without gathering your pieces one by one to add to your picture, you have no idea what you are doing. The books I wrote were specific to people in a place where I knew them well. They too were trying to make sense of things, but because man and tradition prevailed, they struggled. I too, as Yeshua did, tried to give them pieces and guidance to try and build the puzzles, but I can't make them put it together.

Truth is a very solid word. When we stand in our truth, there is nothing else like it. It is a prevailing white light. It is sustained unconditional love. I began to know things as you do, I began to trust, I didn't care about outcomes. I knew if it was meant to be, it would happen because that was my truth. I began to understand that people throughout centuries continue to lose the love of self because we don't know our truth.

Yeshua knew that I was watching him. He knew that my energy, my vibration at the time, was not one of evil, and yet I was, what you call, "performing evil deeds." What my surface-self was doing was following a different guidebook.

[Andrea's comments, He showed me an enclosed enlarged guidebook, in reference to man's laws, that he was following.]

I believed in different men. Your guidebook is your guidebook. At any time, you pick up any book to be your guidebook, and ask that the truth be revealed. Many teachers, many masters, many guides have written down things. And not all things can resonate, but truth will be told. You will find truth in maybe one sentence out of a whole book, but that adds a piece to your puzzle. I encourage you, as I have for many people throughout centuries, by my book and who I am, to never stop seeking who you are. We are evolving souls.

You, Andrea, have been doing very well in teaching this. Step up your truth so you bring out the truth in others. Not faster, not quicker – stronger. I adore your people because as centuries have gone by, we chose to come back and to learn this truth in ourselves. Therefore, I am available to help bring truth to light and to love. Peace be to you. - Paul

Peter shared the following after the message after Paul concluded.

The Apostle Peter

Denying our Truth

My topic is about denying the truth. I was a man that had many wants and wishes, and I usually got what I wanted. I was what you would call "charming," and I had a way with people, especially the ladies. I was enjoying my life and I thought I had it pretty good. When I would sit out on my boat alone fishing, fishing for the fish, waiting for the fish, sometimes even asking the fish to come, I would contemplate things about life. I too have the thought as you, Andrea, as I sat out there, that there had to be more to this life than what I was experiencing. I enjoyed being what you call "the life of the party". I had fun, and when this man approached me, I knew there was something in his eyes that spoke truth to me. My thoughts were rampant. How could he know all of this in this lifetime? Where did he go to get this? What makes him special? "I understand your proverbial two-year-old description that you so often use."

[This is a phrase I use often in my sessions about how we must constantly ask questions about ourselves things like: Why is this happening? What is this showing up for? How can this help me?]

I too had those questions about him. And, because I lived a very free life, my thought was why not? Why not see what he has to offer? So, I decided to go with him on these journeys. He was very interesting to me. He was a very gentle, kind man and it seemed as if even the insects would know he was coming and move out of his way. At times, I felt I was the observer watching how he reacted to people. Watching how he did things, how he didn't do things, and that made me more intrigued to find out more about him. I learned many hard examples of truth about myself in experiencing some hardships, some arguments, and some faint moments. You would say I was the one who would go out and have to experience these things for myself to actually believe it was true. I would agree with that. And so, because I put myself in these situations to be challenged, yes I denied him because I didn't want to die at that moment. Yes, I excused myself from Gentiles, and what you would call lower class citizens today, because I was taught they were beneath me. Some of the things that happened were not written in all of the books. I tested people, I went out of my way to start arguments because I had to know my own truth of what I was being shown. I am a visionary like you, Andrea, and when I would sit in my prayers, I would see many things. This also helped me to understand in a greater way. I did not have the knowledge that Paul carried. I did do reading of many books, and so too, Paul and I had the same experience of combining what we knew from old ancient texts to what was being shown to us in a man (Jesus).

You see, your statement, Andrea, about there being no Satan.

[I frequently tell clients there is no Satan, no evil, no devil; that it's our own created fear.]

This is partly why Yeshua called me Satan [Mathew 16:23] because it is actually denying ourselves of truth. And out of that fear, we created your so-called Satan being. At least I am not a doubting Thomas, I do not want a title before my name like that. Thank goodness they don't call me denying Peter. I own that because I fully embraced my human side and I challenged it, and when Yeshua transfigured and came back, the truth merged with my soul side. I became one. I understood there was no death. I understand the temporary time that we choose to have on this so-called Earth. I too, like Paul and John, have chosen to stay available for many to ask and access for guidance and support. I too understand that this book that many read, they call it "Gospel", but the true teachings of Yeshua has, is, and always will be "the truth will set you free." And that, my friend is love. - Peter

There is such a wealth of information here. It serves as eternal reminder that the truth that resides in each of us, can only be known if we first want to know, and second if we relentlessly search for it. And when we find it, we must be willing to take all the actions necessary to live a life in total alignment with our truth—no matter what.

So many big changes came into my life in a very short window of time over the last two years. This has been because of my relentless seeking of truth. It would be a lie to say it was easy, but it would also be a lie to say it was hard. All of these growth experiences have contributed to the well-being of my soul. Some scientific research around the topic of happiness suggests that people are not very good at predicting what will bring them happiness. This is because, in actuality, we do know what will bring us happiness, but we rarely stand strong in truth and, therefore, are inaccurate in our choices. The level of accuracy can only be measured by truth. In other words, you can only be as accurate as you are truthful with yourself.

People miss the mark because they deny their truth. By example, Paul and Peter both observed Jesus, but they kept their distance until they were directly confronted with a truth that could no longer be ignored. Our goal, in truth, is to not create such extreme circumstances to uncover our truth. Our current civilization is so advanced, yet we are fraught with disease, war, emotional distress, and suffering. This is all because we have become so uncomfortable standing in our truth.

My truth is not your truth. In reading this book, I want you to find the pieces of the puzzle that resonate with your truth and leave the remainder for others. You must walk your own path, as I must walk mine. Choosing a life of truth is more than being honest, or being in integrity in your everyday interactions. Choosing a life of truth is about standing up for your soul's glorification, and continually living in a way that supports your soul's growth. No matter what.

Choices

Now that the importance of love and truth has been emphasized, it seems appropriate to look at one other concept that is vital for a bliss-filled future. We are ready to look at how opportunities to express pure love continuously manifest in everything we choose. This requires us to understand the concept of mind control in a way that goes beyond anything we've ever imagined. To recognize every situation as a choice, in every circumstance, no matter what the outer appearance.

Recognizing that we choose everything in our lives is a bit disconcerting at first. If you read *My Invincible Life* from the start, you may have already taken an inventory of your life. The idea that every circumstance-be it joyous and/or painful-is our choice, has been a profound realization in my journey. I have replaced questions such as "Why is this happening to me?" with the more useful question of "What is this here to show me?" Once the lesson is clear, I can consciously choose to manifest more of that which is joyful and move past that which no longer serves me. The trick is in recognizing it is all a matter of choice.

One example can be found living within this book. For several years my knowing has guided me to write this book. As stated previously, I've always known it was three parts, and that I was supposed to share some aspect of my life journey. I've also had a knowing that it is supposed to be published by a publishing company. Many of my spiritual colleagues have self-published and enjoy the benefits and freedoms that go with that option. I had to start the process by taking my book out to publishers and agencies. The process included some early rejection, and this showed me that instead of three books, this would be better as three sections in one book. Later, I was advised that this could be three books if they were published in an e-book format. For now, it is one book, three parts, and self-published.

I know that my work is not going to be accepted by everyone, so I am trusting the right presentation of the collection and the right publishing route will emerge in a way that is the best vibrational match for sharing these messages.

It would have been possible for me to not reach out to publishers or agents, and just sit with this book, hoping one day a publisher would come to me. My knowing suggested that I had to pursue an agent and publisher, letting people know about my book so the right opportunity could show itself. This requires total self-acceptance and willingness to let go of any sense of rejection. Each "no" is one step closer to my "yes." NO = next opportunity. There was a time in the past when I would push back on my knowing and try to control the circumstances. This was certainly true for my marriage. I tried to make it work even when I knew it wasn't right. With this book series, I have learned to follow my guidance, even when the path is filled with uncertainty. Understanding that everything is a divinely guided choice allows me to accept things as they are, without limits or controls.

We are conditioned as a society to look outside of ourselves for how to think and believe. The American dream is go to work, take vacations, buy the house, get the cars, and then retire, as if that alone is our purpose in life. Yet there are so many people who are so unhappy because they are living somebody else's idea of the dream. We look to churches to tell us how to interpret the Bible and bring us fulfillment and answers. We look to television to give us a false identity of what life is like, whether dramas or comedies. We look to the government to tell us how certain timelines are to be followed for education, career, and retirement. We look to media and marketing to tell us what we like, what we want, and what we need. They tell us the "best" thing to get in every aspect of our lives. We look forward to going on vacation so we can check out, do what we want to do, and see what we want to see. Shouldn't *that* be the way our life is all the time? Every day is supposed feel like a vacation.

In spirituality, we tend to seek out gurus, teachers, leaders, mentors—anyone to tell us what *they* think we need to know. Certainly my path included studying a variety of different seemingly enlightened thought leaders. This practice of looking outside of ourselves spiritually is no different than looking to television, government, or media for answers. It is time to stop looking outwardly.

You hold all the answers within. It's funny that, as I am writing this book, I make a living sharing messages from Spirit. The irony of this truth is that one of Spirit's messages is that you don't need messages from me or others. You are already getting them: from nature, from all livings things, from signs on trucks, from listening in on nearby conversations, from hearing voices in your head that are not your own, from having a memory flash after you ask question, from having a memory trigger arise from song lyrics or a familiar color, or just knowing something. The messages are constant. This is all Spirit (angels, archangels, guides, galactic beings, fairies, and so on). They are all getting messages to us; we just need to get better at being more aware.

My nature is to be rebellious. Rebelliousness is a part of who I am. As a Taurus, I can relate to the analogy of being a "bull in a china shop." I have a tendency to shake up, or rattle, the status quo. Think about it. Are you really content in your life, with your choices to have the house, the car, the vacation? Or are you actually just allowing circumstances, people, or society to tell you what you want and need? We are constantly doing things that are outwardly supposed to be satisfying, but they are not really what we want to do.

In the beginning of our human existence, we tell others what we need and want. But somewhere along the way we are told to stop asking for what we want. We are told to follow others' rules, routines, and guidelines. We're under the care of people who have forgotten what they really want, and so we learn to stop wanting for ourselves. We tend think of *rebellion* as a fighting word, but really it is a word of self-acceptance. When we rebel against things that don't feel good or right, we are honoring our authentic truth. My inner rebel speaks from the place of my knowing. She has kept close to the truth for my entire life. I hated people trying to brush my hair or tell me what to wear.

Once I even went from blonde to jet black. It was my childlike way of standing in my truth in any way I could.

It is time for all of us to come out of the hypnotic state of mind control. Do you hear a voice, have a gut feeling, or just a sense in your mind that speaks from your inner knowing? This is your truth and must be acknowledged. All along, my journey has been about finding the truth. Not your truth. Not telling you what your truth is. Not even giving you your truth. This book has been about me finding my truth, and in sharing that I was able to overcome the lies of victim thinking and lies such as "Other people caused my pain (family, abusers, friends)" or "The pain is too much to handle" or "I was dealt a bad hand (got the short end of the stick) in life." Overcoming all these lies has led me to live in my truth. No matter what.

There Is No Pain

My truth about people who seemingly caused me pain is that they were a part of my journey of learning. In "My Invincible Truth," I wrote about how I was raped multiple times in my childhood. I have come to understand those experiences differently now. In my younger years, my false belief was that I "deserved" what happened to me because I was somehow bad or wrong. In my adult years, I tried to pretend those things simply never occurred. In my truth, I now understand those experiences are not bad or good; they are just my experiences. By removing labels (good or bad) and cutting the cord of false beliefs, I have found peace in my heart. I have love for the abusers. I am now able to thank them for fulfilling their part of my soul's contract.

Gratitude has become a significant part of my daily living. Every situation that arises, joyful or painful, leads me to thank my higher self and my guides. I find that I am able to move through what may have been deemed difficult situations fairly effortlessly. I still feel frustration, sadness, and even curiosity about why things may be happening. I find myself saying, "Everything happens for a reason, and that reason is here to support me." In some situations, I understand that everything is happening for a reason, and I acknowledge that I may not understand the reason in the moment, or even like that it is happening, but I know it is for my higher learning. So, I keep walking through whatever it is so I can grow.

My truth about pain is that there is no pain. While writing this book, it may have looked to others as if I were experiencing pain just this week. The outside world may see my sadness or upset as painful. However, I am able to see now that it is not pain causing these emotions; it is resistance. When my soul resists a lesson, it appears painful. It shows up in a myriad of emotions, clueing me into to something my soul wants me to get.

It is actually painful to lower our vibration. When we are in the higher vibration of love and gratitude and then drop down to frustration and fear, it physically hurts our body. Then, our emotions let our ego take over. Our hearts can hurt. It is important to go through the mind/body process and release the hurt so there is no more attachment.

One example is when loved ones have crossed over and people are very sad and emotionally heartbroken. When the crossed-over soul comes through to talk to their living loved ones, they carry a higher vibration of love and support. So, while there may be tears in talking with souls who have crossed over, the healing/growing process starts as well, because your vibration rises with the understanding that they are not completely gone. Physically they are gone, but their soul lives on. The sooner someone allows their mind and body to accept what has happened, the quicker they are able to heal/grow and move forward. This is partially why the grief journey looks so different for each and every person.

We grieve the loss of many things in our lives, yet with most of those losses we try to act as if it is not happening, or not causing us to hurt, when in reality, any evolutionary step could have a grief element. For example, when being born, a soul grieves dropping into a dense body. Even changing schools, a child grieves the loss of teachers or friends. When changing jobs, workers grieve the loss of familiarity. When getting married, people grieve the loss of their single life. With divorce, people grieve the loss of coupling. The loss of a loved one is just another example of something we grieve. All of these examples are the same in that they require us to acknowledge that, when they happen, it is not as devastating as we've been told. Instead, if we choose, these events can fully support our soul's growth. We can choose to understand it to be happening either for us or against us. I choose to see that everything is happening for our best and highest good.

Some people will read through "My Invincible Truth" and think, *Wow, that's really raw*. I look at my story and think, *Wow, I am really blessed*. I was dealt, and continue to be dealt, a hand that serves my best and highest good. We are all dealt our own special hand. I am not to here to tell anyone what their hand should look or feel like. I am sharing the truth that has freed me to live my best possible life. By understanding the situations in front of me as being here to support me, by my choice I am able to trust and find the joy in everything that happens, almost exactly as it happens. No matter what.

A Message from Muhammed:

Divinity by Design

We know what divinity is. We come from the other dimension into this one knowing what divinity is. And we have completely forgotten at some early stage. We are created to be divine beings; we are by design.

Design (definition) – To prepare the preliminary sketch or plans for a work to be executed. Plan the form and structure of—to INTEND for a definite purpose. To form or conceive in the mind. To assign in thought or intention.

"Come unto me like little children" Jesus

Divinity – quality of being divine. God. A divine being. A being having divine attributes. God like character. Supreme excellence.

It is so easy to think of children as open and accepting and not knowing right from wrong, so we let them explore. They begin with a selfishness and we teach their knowing right out of them.

In divinity by design. We are here to experience GOD as we so design. We begin with a sketch and design as we go.

If we are truly pre-designed already knowing this divine nature; then I chose to have all of these experiences and then awaken to my divinity. I knew by design that when I started remembering who I was that there was something bigger. I could feel that there was something bigger, that I was a larger part of the humanity on earth. Every country I have ever gone too I have always felt very comfortable – Greece, India, Croatia, Mexico, Italy – we all carry these human attributes in us so we start connecting on a soul level.

If there is no divine purpose/path/contract and we come here to separate ourselves from the One, it's so we can have these experiences for our soul's growth. As humanity being all One, we continue to have soul's growth, and then we are also continuing to help others remember who they are. So as a whole, we are love, truth, peace, and bliss; and in separation we are without memory. We have just forgotten and it pisses a lot of people off. We keep coming back, reincarnating to prove those who are stuck in the human experience of separation can remember. The only thing is that when we come back to help, we have to become separate to do so. The cycle of separation continues until we strengthen the remembering.

Choosing to have these horrific experiences shows humanity we can go through anything and still remember who we are. Hitler came to show that people can come together in strong compassionate love for one another. On the other side, Hitler is an angel *(no specifics as to light or dark).* In his lifetime he communed with Angels and Galactic beings in his subconscious and in his knowing. The angels and galactics did create his actions, HE chose to use prolific tactics.

We came together with other countries to overcome what we perceived as evil, it brought us together.

As much as Gandhi came and showed humanity love and light, Hitler committed to the experience of demonstration of oneness. That is why we build monuments to remind us of how strong we are as love beings.

[Muhammed, a very light hearted energy, and he is showing me that his book is so distorted and misunderstood, and that he was writing so that humanity would continue to fight for each other, not against. Instead, they believed it was to further separate. He was talking about a unified humanity. He compares himself to Solomon. Even Solomon got mad at the people because of their own stupidity and getting to the point of not thinking for themselves.]

He wrote from a viewpoint of frustration at the people wanting to stay in a lower vibration. The Quran is just like the Bible, there are other books that were not included and his words have been changed in certain texts. He understands and for that it is overcoming and remembering that the Islam faith, that those who read it, understand that it really is about love. Just as in the Bible, Christians are supposed to be Christ like yet some of the deepest rooted Christians in the Bible have a hatred for other humans based on a misunderstanding of context due to missing writings or changes made erroneously. Another way to say "divinity by design" is "love by agenda."

[A Sacramento artist, Jill Layton, painted a picture that Muhammed refers to in the following text.]

The Samo picture [see below] shows that it is the human brain and skull and all of the things that permeate within. What we are doing to ourselves is that we are opening our 3rd eye and have attached this carrot in front of us. We all hang a carrot in front of ourselves and the ONE finger is wanting to reach out to be one with the knowing. And instead, what's happening around is all that is inside. And that it is split down the middle with male colors on one side and female colors on the other and shows the dualistic nature of man. Thank you for listening and I appreciate your willingness to write down words in truth because all humanity is "divinity by design."

Understanding many paths as the tree of life. Many ascended masters (Buddha) spoke about nature because nature has all of the answers in it. – Muhammed

Jill Layton, "For SAMO", 2013. Acrylic on canvas, 24"x 36"

Noticing and Synchronicity

I don't know why you picked up this book, but I do know that because you picked up this book, there is a message for you here, just as there are messages everywhere. You may think that now is a time for a shift—in you, in your environment, or in the world. Change is the last thing we need; what our souls seek is truth. The one constant is always change.

Over the last few days, I have noticed birds acting strangely. I've seen spiral bird formations; for instance, as I drove past a refuse area, there were close to a thousand birds spiraling in the air. This is an area I have driven past for over twenty years and I have never witnessed anything like this before. That same day, I stopped at someone's house and two doves were in front of the home. As I approached the doves, they didn't fly away with what might be considered a typical fleeing response. Instead they just walked a bit to the side and only when the occupant opened the door did they fly away. I also saw two hawks flying with multiple turkey vultures in spiral formation. This is noteworthy because typically these birds are predatory competitors.

Today, when I was driving home, there was another massive spiral formation of what appeared to be turkey vultures so high in the air that had I not had my glasses on, I would not have seen them. And more were headed toward them until they chose to disappear toward the stormy clouds. It seemed as though they fell into a portal. I watched them, and then I didn't see them anywhere. Driving on, a blue jay flew down toward my car and flew alongside me. After looking at the bird in such close proximity to my car, I suddenly noticed that the song "Time for Me to Fly" by REO Speedwagon was playing on the car stereo.

As I sat down to work on edits for this book series this evening, I shared my story about the birds with my collaborator. I asked my guides to help me understand the meaning of all of the bird sightings and the unusual behavior being exhibited. I asked, "What am I missing?

Why are they behaving this way right now?" I then picked up my cell phone and read a meme of the day from Sara Landon that read:

Spread your wings and fly, see where the winds of change will take you. What you need will be there. You have beautiful gifts and you have the whole universe here to support you.

Thank goodness for this guidance. By taking notice of everything around me, I was able to fully take in the message of freedom as being an essential section of this book still to be written.

Freedom & Followership

Channeled with Jesus and the Apostles

We want you to know that you can be a follower and be free. It is in freedom that you are able to choose the messengers who most align with your truth. It is in followership that you are able to grow in your truth and expand it for universal well-being. We know that it sounds confusing to have both freedom and followership. Yet it is essential that they go together. For far too many years there has been suffering on the earth because followership has been taken to an extreme and individuals have lost their sense of freedom; they have lost their own truth. We know that the biblical stories may seem to take followership to an extreme, but that is not the case. If you interpret the writings as they were intended, you will see that my followers were simply choosing what aligned with their truth. Those that did not have the alignment did not follow, and that was fine. At the last supper there was much discussion about who was my favorite disciple and John laid his head on me and said, "I am." What Scripture tells us is that John and Jesus were close; they had an understanding. John had this love already within him; therefore, it was very easy for him to see the love that Jesus had. So, there was no favoritism; there was just a stronger knowing within John. Love permeates through all doubt, negativity, and conversation. It is a state of being, not something to be achieved, to go and find, or to try to dominate. In the state of being love, we are complete. There is no other definition of freedom. So you see, freedom and followership must go together. For in followership we grow and expand in our truth.

We must first know our truth and seek messengers who help us understand it in more depth and then go beyond the limits of our own thinking.

Conclusion

Societally, we appear to have things a bit backward. We strive for acceptance in everything, failing to recognize that our differences make us unique and wonderful. Our quirks and craziness make us fun and authentic. The life-marks on our bodies make us beautiful. Some call them wrinkles, some call them scars, and some call them laugh lines. Whatever we are putting out to the world, it is essential that we come to accept who we are and what we offer. It is not intended for everyone; it is intended for the right ones—the vibrational match that encourages us to grow ourselves spiritually.

I didn't change from the experiences I had, and *they* didn't change me. I didn't change when I became a Christian. Nor did I change when I started down the spiritual path. It has always been an awakening. I am more fully awake; I am not different, nor did I change. I remembered my authentic self. And now I love me. I love how I am. I love who I am. I love all aspects of me. This allows me to be as free as a bird, to soar low or high.

As I have become my authentic self, my vibration has expanded. And with that, external circumstances appear different. Relationships with family, friends, and even clients continue to evolve. As people witness my vibrational expansion, they each have their own perspective on my choices. My responsibility is to stand in my truth. If I find I am triggered by someone's reactions to my choices, then it is my responsibility to clear the emotional cord causing the pain of resistance. It is not my role to try and shift their experience or beliefs; nor is it my role to save them from hurt or pain. It is about accepting things the way they are, with a mindset of pure love, even if outwardly it looks or feels awkward for a time.

You may remember from "My Invincible Awakening" that I took a road trip to Montana. While traveling through the mountains, there was a river that ran parallel to the road. At one point along the river, I pulled over to watch some kayakers navigate the fast-moving rapids. One of the kayakers turned completely around and started going upstream. It is hard to conceive how he was able to do this, yet it did not appear as if he were struggling. It was obvious that he was turned in a way that was not in alignment with the current. For a short time, when I was seeking my truth, I felt like that kayaker: strong in perseverance and yet still going against the natural flow. I have awakened to a point in my life where I am no longer the kayaker going against the current—I am the river flowing.

Epilogue

So much has happened since I first started this book in early 2014 after my first separation from my ex-husband. Since then it has evolved and more added to it. Just like life, we are always adding more to our experiences for our growth and expansion.

Throughout this book one could say I have been healing through all my experiences. That we seek to heal our wounds of traumatic experiences. What my guides revealed to me is that we never heal from the inside. Our bodies have the capability to heal. You get a cut, it will heal. When we experience traumatic events in our lives, we grow and expand our soul. We don't heal from the loss of a loved one. We learn to continue growing for our own selves. This made sense to me and I have been sharing this in all my sessions. And I have had my own therapy along with friends who are therapists and there is an agreement with this understanding now. We can try to numb out our experiences to prevent our own soul's growth, but that only stops the human body from feeling the attachment to the experience. Thus, anger, bitterness and/or resentment will set in and stump the soul's growth process. Hence, I use the word healing and I now prefer to use the words growth or expansion.

One of my more profound

My oldest sister, my dad and me

experiences happened in early 2019. In the beginning of this book I mention that I was sexually abused. My sexual abuse began when I was 2 years old by a babysitter, again when I was 7 years old by the next door neighbor couple who was babysitting me and just recently another memory has come forward that I was sexually abused when I was 5 years old for many years and was (probably still is) part of the child pornography syndicate. I know there are pictures and videos of me out there. I can't change the past and I can help others to keep moving forward. To help see that there is good, hope and love on this planet.

As I got older, I became very intrigued hearing stories of sexual abuse, human sex trafficking and child pornography. I realize now that it was because I was one of those children. I always felt a desire to fight for the underdog, but then I had so much anger myself and I was the one inflicting pain on others. I was the underdog and I couldn't fight for myself. Sex trafficking, child abuse, child pornography is rampant all over the world and it must stop. It's not just little girls, it's boys and girls. In my sessions, I hear it from both sides and many a times over. Trauma is trauma and yes, we are here to learn to overcome this and it is something that can be eradicated if we learn that our own experiences are our own and we don't have to inflict that pain onto others.

Writing this book series has taken several years to complete because it fully reflects my past, present, and future in all aspects, conditions, and experiences. Every day I am learning to love myself more and more. I made a conscious choice to know my truth, no matter what. When I made the choice, I had only a slight idea of all that was in store for me—day to day, week to week, month to month.

I chose to really want to know who my authentic self is. I did this consciously, with the understanding that I was choosing it, no matter what. I did not yet know how the awareness would continually shift and bring me more deeply into an awakened state. I did not know the extent of change in family situations and global travel that would open up, or even the nomadic lifestyle that would emerge. I couldn't have imagined all of the different vibrational energies outside the dimension I called my life. As I have moved forward in my truth, I have been introduced to galactic beings, archangels not previously written about, ascended masters, enlightened beings, and so many more. During my childhood, my life looked and felt chaotic. During the time of my marriage, my life looked safe and secure, but my inner world was chaotic. Today, my life looks free and inviting, and I am in bliss. I would do this entire life all over again because it has been exciting, fun, challenging, and expansive; and because I chose it.

It is always my choice, and the words "no matter what" remind me that I *am* choosing this. I choose to fully love myself, to live in truth, no matter what. It is the only reminder I need to give myself each day until it becomes a part of me. Understanding this choice allows me to experience everything from the perspective of my soul's growth and expansion, no matter who is in—or out—of my life. This is healing, if we so choose. This is pure love. No matter what.

One last example of how choice and magic make our lives better happened just recently while on our way to Montana. As we approached Twin Falls, ID we were directed to take a detour due to construction. This was our first visit to this city and we had no clue what to expect. The detour took us all through residential neighborhoods. At one point, we felt like we were lost. We debated about how to proceed; whether we should turn around or keep going through the neighborhoods. We were on an adventure, no matter what, so we decided to keep going. Seconds after affirming our adventure purpose, we emerged onto a main road and an enormous gorge revealed itself. After passing over the gorge in awe, we were so amazed at the size it, we felt compelled to make a U-turn to get a better look at it.

We got out of the car and walked around in separate directions each admiring the scenery. We were there for some time taking it all in. As we joined back up near the car, a white Chevy Suburban with the windows down, blaring *Free Falling* by Tom Petty was approaching. You could hear the tires almost screech onto the dirt road from the sheer speed. I remember thinking as I approached my car, "that is some loud music playing." The SUV came to a screeching halt and the door was flown open. Out comes a woman dressed in all black, black hair and black sunglasses holding a cigarette all the while the song continues to play. She approaches our car and yells, 'which one of you needs a healing?' My travel buddy was already getting in my car when I advised her of the woman's request. I told the woman, "She does," and made my buddy get out and come over. She comes around the car and lifts her arms in the air and places them on the car. Just out of a typical scene watching a suspect being searched. Then the woman has her turn around and away from my car. She then places her hand on my friend's back, lifting the cigarette carrying arm in the air and begins chanting.

Unbeknownst to the woman was the fact that when I picked up my traveling buddy, she had a couple pillows to sit with due to ongoing lower back and hip issues. As the woman was behind my friend doing her thing, I got in front and started lifting the energy up and through her body. Helping to release any resistance and to allow for any movement to happen/heal. As the woman came to a close of her chanting, she drops her arm and starts making a rather interesting grunting noise, shaking her arm and still holding her cigarette arm in the air. She doesn't say anything as she proceeds back to her Suburban, when I ask her if I could give her a hug. She agrees and gives us both one and all the while, the song is still playing in the background. She barrels out of the path yelling out her window, "Woo-hoo ... woo-hoo ... woo-hoo!!" We get into my car and my friend crosses her legs for the first time in almost a year and says, "I'm healed. I'm good now." We followed to the main route and as she went back over the bridge, she raised her arm up and down and yelled her last "Woo-hoo!" We acknowledged her "woo-hoo" with our own back to her and headed our own way. We promptly saw the sign leading us back to the freeway proceeding North. We were once again on our way to Montana.

This was one of several amazing experiences we had on the trip and I wanted to share this one in particular because a stranger in another state heard her truth. She knew that someone needed a healing and she took the time to listen, take action and have her own amazing experience with us. Magic and Miracles. We should be experiencing magic and miracles every day. Not as a phenomenon. As every day, all-day experiences. This is the game of Life and if we aren't having fun and enjoying this life then I ask you to ask yourself ... what am I here for? What I am doing for myself? What is my life about? You already know the answers ... they are within. Trust and listen to your amazing self. You got this!

A Final Channeling

While writing this book, I channeled an entity that wanted to be called "The Ursula." She asked me to share this message:

The Ursula

We [humans] procreate, not to make more of our human selves, but to procreate on a soul level. We have neglected to remember nature. We have forgotten to be continually reminded how nature procreates itself. We lose that element about how all these things create and procreate. That which bring us joy, bliss, and substantial wealth is not from utilizing nature [she showed me logging trucks], but by being in nature.

The wealth of understanding, the wealth of love, the wealth of knowledge, the wealth in law—nature carries all balance, all ebb and flow, and all law. The vast ocean is nature, and all things created within it, some of which you do not see. The things that you have been shown, that you do see, are all the same nature, whether under the water or not [the earth].

You see, there is no separation between these two, water and earth. And yet one is the yin and one is the yang. The nature in water is the feminine energy. The nature outside of the water [earth] is the masculine energy. Trees grow, they become big and strong, they protect. Birds put their nests in the tress because they know the trees will protect. Animals burrow into the earth because they know it will protect. Caves protect man and animal. This is the male energy.

The ocean is the rising feminine energy. The need to be near water is the element hidden within—hidden because we forget what is below the water; we only see the surface. She [water] is wanting to rise up in a greater way. As she produces and gives of herself in many different ways from all the living organisms under the water, she also gives back to the atmosphere to help produce water that brings life to all, whether it be in nature or man. There is power in her waves; vibration resonates through water and can go for miles and miles. This is what we are here to do. As this feminine energy is rising, we are to send out this vibration of love.

We don't die from the water; we drown because we give up the fight. We drown because we forget to relax and just float, just be in the water. It may sound contradictory to fight and float to survive in the water, but the fighting is within yourself; the struggle to just be in the water versus trying to survive what is coming at you. Water is a force to be reckoned with when she is mad. And she is mad because we are fighting against this feminine energy.

It is not to say that a woman cannot do the same thing as a man, but why does she want to compare herself to him? She is her own unique individual person who can do whatever she wants, because she wants to do it. You are getting the understanding of this truth. There is truth in nature, just as there is truth in you. There is love in nature.

You always speak of this Mother Bear that would do anything for her cubs because that is love and that is her truth. Those truths will also produce thoughts for your fellow man of love, of goodness, of truth. Just as in land you have Mother Bear, in the ocean we have the same. Whales protect their young; dolphins protect their young. They are a loving community; they understand the laws of nature; it is within [she showed me how they use their knowing to travel and protect each other]. This is what humans are lacking right now. So please tell this story [she showed me women converging on a beach because this feminine energy is rising]. Take in this natural, innate talent, ability, and sensuality. I am many shades of blue for speaking the truth [she showed me the throat chakra, whose energy is in seeking and speaking your authentic truth]. Stand in one. Thank you. - The Ursula.

References

Robert Plant, 'Big Log' from the Album 'The Principle of Moments' (1983)

Pink Floyd, 'Comfortably Numb' from the Album 'The Wall' (1979)

Marvin Gaye, 'Sexual Healing' from the Album 'Midnight Love' (1982)

NIV Holy Bible (updated 2011). United States: Zondervan

REO Speedwagon, 'Time for Me to Fly' from the Album 'You Can Tune a Piano, but You Can't Tuna Fish' (1978)

Tom Petty, 'Free Falling' from the Album 'Full Moon Fever' (1989)

Photo credit of Shiva Lingham provided by Devipuram
http://www.devipuram.com/

Photo credit of 'For SAMO' provided by the artist of the painting, Jill Layton

Cover design: Natasha Clawson, www.aspireenco.com

Cover photo: In Her Image Photography, www.InHerImagePhoto.com

Books That Have Added Awareness to My Life

The Four Agreements, Don Miguel Ruiz

You Can Heal Your Life, Louise Hay

Emissary of Light, James Twyman

This Thing Called You, Ernest Holmes

The Moses Code, James Twyman

Science of Mind, Ernest Holmes

The Hidden Mystery of the Bible, Jack Ensign Addington

The Bible (King James Version)

Complete Jewish Bible, David H. Stern

Truth Heals, Deborah King

Be Your Own Shaman, Deborah King